This is the first comprehensive study of Brecht's *Mother Courage*. Peter Thomson locates the sources of the play in Brecht's experience and heritage, and provides a detailed account of Brecht's own production with the newly forming Berliner Ensemble in 1949. Thomson then explores how the play has been transmitted in the English-speaking theatre from Joan Littlewood's production with the Theatre Workshop company in 1955 to the Royal National Theatre, with Diana Rigg as Mother Courage, in 1995.

The book also examines such influential interpretations as those by William Gaskill, Judi Dench and Glenda Jackson in the English theatre, and by Herbert Blau and Richard Schechner in America. Seminal productions in France and the Germanies are also discussed. A final chapter highlights the new urgency of the text in light of the wars in former Yugoslavia, and closes with an account of a triumphant staging in Uganda.

BRECHT

MOTHER COURAGE
AND HER CHILDREN

PLAYS IN PRODUCTION

Series editor: Michael Robinson

BRECHT

MOTHER COURAGE AND HER CHILDREN

∗

PETER THOMSON
University of Exeter

∗

with a conclusion by
VIV GARDNER
University of Manchester

CAMBRIDGE
UNIVERSITY PRESS

PUBLISHED BY THE PRESS SYNDICATE OF THE UNIVERSITY OF CAMBRIDGE
The Pitt Building, Trumpington Street, Cambridge CB2 1RP, United Kingdom

CAMBRIDGE UNIVERSITY PRESS
The Edinburgh Building, Cambridge CB2 2RU, United Kingdom
40 West 20th Street, New York, NY 10011–4211, USA
10 Stamford Road, Oakleigh, Melbourne 3166, Australia

First published 1997

Printed in the United Kingdom at the University Press, Cambridge

Typeset in Adobe Garamond 10.75/14, in QuarkXpress™ [SE]

A catalogue record for this book is available from the British Library

Library of Congress cataloguing in publication data
Thomson, Peter, 1938–
Brecht: Mother Courage and her children / Peter Thomson; with a
conclusion by Viv Gardner.
p. cm. – (Plays in production; 5)
Includes bibliographical references and index.
ISBN 0 521 45404 2 (hardback). – ISBN 0 521 59774 9 (paperback)
1. Brecht, Bertolt, 1898–1956. Mutter Courage und ihre Kinder.
2. Brecht, Bertolt, 1898–1956 – Dramatic production. 3. Brecht,
Bertolt, 1898–1956 – Stage history. I. Gardner, Viv. II. Title.
III. Series.
PT2603.R397M928 1997
832'.912 – dc21 97-37706 CIP

ISBN 0 521 45404 2 hardback
ISBN 0 521 59774 9 paperback

I dedicate this book to the
Mystics and Magicians Cricket Club
and to David Gower, who would be
a welcome addition to it.

CONTENTS

ILLUSTRATIONS

GENERAL PREFACE

Volumes in the series Plays in Production take major dramatic texts and examine their transposition, firstly on to the stage and, secondly, where appropriate, into other media. Each book includes concise but informed studies of individual dramatic texts, focusing on the original theatrical and historical context of a play in relation to its initial performance and reception followed by subsequent major interpretations on stage, both under the impact of changing social, political and cultural values, and in response to developments in the theatre generally.

Many of the plays also have been transposed into other media – film, opera, television, ballet – which may well be the form in which they are first encountered by a contemporary audience. Thus, a substantial study of the play-text and the issues it raises for theatrical realisation is supplemented by an assessment of such adaptations as well as the production history, where the emphasis is on the development of a performance tradition for each work, including staging and acting styles, rather than simply the archaeological reconstruction of past performances.

Plays included in the series are all likely to receive regular performance and individual volumes will be of interest to the informed reader as well as to students of theatre history and literature. Each book also contains an annotated production chronology as well as numerous photographs from key performances.

Michael Robinson
University of East Anglia

ACKNOWLEDGEMENTS

I should first acknowledge the generous assistance of Jeanette Hunter, who spent part of her intercalary year in Germany scouring back-numbers of *Theater Heute* for me, and even sent me translations of some of what she found there. My colleagues Christopher McCullough and Lesley Soule were always willing to lend me an ear or a book. Vicki Cooper and Michael Robinson were patient and kind to a fault.

One of the most daunting tasks that confronts an author is the pursuit of illustrations. What I would like particularly to acknowledge is the startling rapidity of response from Andrea Müller of *Theater Heute*, Dr Erdmut Wizisla of the Brecht Archiv, Mrs Ute Eichel of the Berliner Ensemble and Jennie Gardner of the Glasgow Citizens' Theatre. Others who have given permission for the reproduction of photographs, etc. are mentioned in the list of illustrations on p. x.

Writing books is not one of the embarrassingly few things I can do without the encouragement of my wife, Rita. Writing this one, alongside the increasingly strident demands of a rampant bureaucracy, would have been impossible without her. Brecht had his HUAC; I have my HEFCE. In conclusion, then, I acknowledge the exemplary irony with which he met his would-be persecutors. Some of it has rubbed off on me.

A NOTE ON TRANSLATION

There are several published translations of *Mother Courage and Her Children*. The one I have used is Ralph Manheim's, from Volume v of the *Collected Plays* (New York: Vintage Books, 1972), a volume which also contains extracts from the Model Book and many of Brecht's notes on the play. Page references within my text are to that volume.

CHAPTER ONE

SOURCES

Brecht was living in Sweden when, on 1 September 1939, the *Wehrmacht* invaded Poland. Few people at that time had a better right to say 'I told you so.' He had been a vigorous campaigner-in-exile against Nazism, and was uncommonly perceptive about Hitler's tactics and intentions. Until April 1939 he had been living in Denmark, where, in the summer of 1938, he had compiled a sequence of short plays under the general title of *Fear and Misery of the Third Reich*. In this work, as he explained in a letter to the American Guild for German Cultural Freedom,

> I tried to bring out two points which I thought it vital to make known abroad: first, the enslavement, disfranchisement, paralysis of *all* sections of the population under the National Socialist dictatorship (people living in the democracies have far too little concrete knowledge of this); second, the state of mind prevailing in the army of the totalitarian state, which is a cross-section of the population as a whole (to give people outside Germany an idea of the fragility of this war machine).[1]

A concern for the population as a whole (rather than for its social and political leaders) and an urge to expose false myths about military morale characterise much of Brecht's work before and after the writing of *Mother Courage and Her Children*, but in the summer of 1939 he was primarily concerned to warn his Scandinavian hosts about Hitler's land-lust. It was the fear of imminent occupation that had driven him out of Denmark, and during the early weeks of his residence on the island of Lidingö, near Stockholm, he wrote for the workers' theatre in Copenhagen a one-act political cartoon. *Dansen* is a deliberately crude allegory of the Nazi plan to annex Denmark.

Also in Lidingö that summer he wrote a companion piece for Sweden, which was staged in Stockholm under the title of *What Is the Price of Iron?* Living in a country whose language he neither spoke nor understood, Brecht was much occupied with thoughts of war.

In the desolate aftermath of the invasion of Poland, Brecht abandoned work on *The Good Person of Szechwan* and, in about five weeks, completed a first draft of *Mother Courage*. The immediate inspiration was a story in Johan Ludvig Runeberg's *Tales of a Subaltern*, which he had heard from the Swedish actress Naima Wifstrand. It was always important to Brecht that his present circumstance should find expression in his writing. When he abandoned projects, it was usually because he had lost faith in their contemporaneity. They no longer spoke for him *now*. Runeberg's story of the camp-following Lotte Svärd, who survives precariously by supplying essential provisions to war-worn soldiers, alerted Brecht to the historical connection between his native and adoptive countries. Never before, and only now since Gustavus Adolphus's powerful intervention in the Thirty Years War, had the fortunes of Sweden (and the unsung segment of its population that formed the Swedish army) and the divided landmass of Germany been so interdependent. For Brecht, the precipitate writing of *Mother Courage* in the autumn of 1939 was the completion of a project begun with *What is the Price of Iron?* His intention was that Wifstrand would play Mother Courage and Helene Weigel, who spoke no Swedish, the specially created part of dumb Kattrin. 'Socialism', Brecht insisted to the more grandiosely idealistic Hermann Greid, 'is nothing but a collection of projects on the part of the proletariat.'[2]

If the initial impetus for the writing of *Mother Courage* was provided by the story of a Scandinavian survivor, the true provenance of the play is German. It was in the divided principalities of seventeenth-century 'Germany' that the hungry troops were most frequently quartered during the dragging winters of the Thirty Years War; and a sense of national pain, of a country whose urge to unity was wickedly frustrated, of a people constrained and disregarded, is classically sited there. Brecht had witnessed the outcome of the German counter-attack in Europe at the end of World War I. As a pacifist in the 1930s, he had recognised with horror the imminence of a second counter-attack, and the consequent folly of appeasing Hitler. As a student of history – the subject which, with religion, had most fired his boyhood imagination – and a political interventionist, he could not detach the past from the present. Runeberg's story of the sutler, Lotte Svärd, opened windows into both the Thirty Years War and the imminent 1940s. Like many of his fellow-exiles, Brecht never truly left Germany. He was obsessed by it.

Although the writing of accurate history was never Brecht's purpose, a reading of *Mother Courage* is enhanced by some familiarity with the confused motives and priorities of the Thirty Years War. C. V. Wedgwood's classic account of it was first published in 1938. Twenty-five years and a world war later, she wrote in the Foreword to a new edition:

> The dismal course of this war still seems to me to be an object
> lesson on the dangers and disasters which can arise when men of
> narrow hearts and little minds are in high places.[3]

The conflict that had arisen in 1618 as a dispute over the kingship of Bohemia, and that was sustained for three decades, with falling and rising intensity, by the associated rivalries the original dispute spawned, finally petered out in 1648, with the still-peremptory struggle for supremacy between Spanish Hapsburgs and French Bourbons unresolved. The throne of Bohemia had, at the outset, served as a pretext for a trial of strength between the Protestant Reformation and the Catholic Counter-Reformation. By the end, the two greatest Catholic powers in Europe were squaring up to each other. This was not, that is to say, one war, but a series of small wars, some consequent on each other, some simultaneous. The common factor was that victory usually went to the generals who kept their troops best provisioned. These are the 'heroes' of conventional history: Gustavus Adolphus on the Protestant side, Wallenstein on the Catholic. Tilly, whose private life was governed by moral rigour and a devotion to the Virgin Mary, was too ill-supplied to contain the pillaging urge of his armies, and has therefore had to carry the blame for the atrocities that followed the capture of Magdeburg in 1631. Mansfeld, a mercenary general in command of a mercenary army, succeeded only so long as his suppliers kept faith with him. Captured soldiers were easily enlisted in the armies of their better-stocked captors. Priests and pastors were especially liable to victim-isation, since the war's religious origin, though often dimly remembered, was never entirely forgotten. Cooks were popular so long as there was food, but sacrificial lambs when it ran out. (The Chaplain in *Mother Courage* is a frightened man, as ready to turn his coat as was the Vicar of Bray, and the Cook's improbable name is Lamb.) Not military tactics, but the provision of food, was the guiding consideration of warfare. Wedgwood cites the recorded comment of a sutler – it might have been Lotte Svärd or Anna Fierling – after the signing of the Peace of Westphalia: 'I was born in war. I have no home, no country and no friends, war is all my wealth and now whither shall I go?'[4]

Brecht would have known the history of his own home-city of Augsburg. At the outbreak of the Thirty Years War, this was one of the 'free cities' of the principalities, by some accounts the greatest Lutheran city of all, but perilously placed in Bavaria, whose Elector, Maximilian, was one of the richest and most constant suppliers of the Imperial (Catholic) armies. In 1629, when Wallenstein forced on the city Ferdinand II's Edict of Restitution, Augsburg was forbidden to exercise Protestant forms of worship and its Lutheran ministers were exiled. Three years later Gustavus Adolphus entered the city in triumph, to the rapturous welcome of stubbornly Protestant Augsburgers. Within six months Gustavus Adolphus was dead, and in 1635, after a six-month siege by the Imperial army, Augsburg sur-rendered to Catholicism again. The city, whose population in 1620 had stood at 48,000, was reduced to 21,000 in 1650.[5] In this decline, Augsburg was representative of the German principalities as a whole. A population of twenty-one million in 1618 had sunk to less than fourteen million by 1648.

Two classics of German literature lie, with Runeberg's *Tales of a Subaltern*, behind *Mother Courage*. The earlier is Hans Jacob Christoffel von Grimmelshausen's *Simplicissimus*, a sprawling picaresque novel whose narrator becomes uncomprehendingly embroiled in the Thirty Years War. Its graphic description of atrocities, delivered often with a disturbing blandness, forces home to the reader Grimmelshausen's horrified recollection of his war-experience. *Simplicissimus* was published in 1669, when the German territories were still rebuilding. In the following year Grimmelshausen brought out the first of its sequels, *Trutz-Simplex*. The sub-title relates it to Brecht: 'Life-story of the arch-swindler and trouble-maker Courage'. *Trutz-Simplex* shows, most importantly, something that Brecht might have made of the story of Mother Courage, but elected not to. In *Simplicissimus* we saw the untrained wild boy – as 'natural' almost as Mowgli or Tarzan/Greystoke – newly minted by the deviousness of the Thirty Years War. By the end he no longer merits the nickname, simplest of simpletons, that gives the book its title. In the sequel he has a liaison with the adventuress Courage, who eventually admits that she has tricked him into believing himself the father of her child. She then tells him the story of her extraordinary life: how, disguised as a page, she served a young captain, became his mistress and married him on his death-bed; how, after further liaisons with a count and an ambassador, she married a captain of dragoons and fought alongside him in battle; how, when her husband was killed, she was first courted and then whipped by a handsome lieutenant; how, when the lieutenant deserted her, she fought on and was personally responsible for the capture of a major; how she learned from her old nurse that she was of noble birth; how she married a third captain, whom she lost in the Danish campaign; how she was put in charge of prisoners, among whom was the major she had captured; how their relationship, fondly begun, culminated in horrific physical abuse, from which she was rescued by a Danish captain; how the gentle Dane took her to his castle, where he cherished her lovingly; how his jealous relations drove her out, forcing her to return to Germany in poverty; how her next lover, a common soldier, was executed for killing a corporal who lusted after her; how she then paired with a musketeer, accompanying him when his regiment was sent to Italy; how she there survived by setting up as a *vivandière*; how she returned to Germany, where she married her fourth captain; and how, after his death in battle, she came to the spa town where she and Simplicissimus are now together. We later learn that her final husband is a gipsy, and that she ends her days as a gipsy queen.

It might be argued that traces of Grimmelshausen's Courage remain in the sheer capacity to survive exhibited by Brecht's, as well as in the multiple fathers of her children. But there is no hint of noble birth or of social mobility in Brecht's Anna Fierling. She is a *vivandière* for life, not in a picaresque episode merely. There is more of Grimmelshausen's Courage in Yvette Pottier than in Mother Courage herself. What has been insufficiently noticed, though, is the effect on Brecht's dramaturgy in this play of the picaresque novel as a genre. Grimmelshausen's Simplicissimus, more completely than his Courage, is a war-created rogue, a *pícaro* of the kind who first appeared in fiction as Lazarillo de Tormes, in 1554. More often acted upon than active, the *pícaro* survives on his wits, cheating cheats in one episode and death in the next. The reader is on his side because he is never a villain except through the circumstances of a villainous world. Wherever he goes, and he tends to travel widely, he meets trouble, and it is through wit and energy, not through a firmness of moral purpose, that he survives.

The episodic nature of picaresque fiction is emphasised in Grimmelshausen's narrative by his chapter-headings. We may take as exemplary the anticipatory titles of Chapter 27 in *Trutz-Simplex*:

> Courage's husband is killed in battle. She herself escapes on her mule, meets a troop of gipsies and is taken by their Lieutenant for his wife. She foretells the future to a young lady in love, robbing her of her jewels the while. But her success is short-lived. She is soundly beaten and made to give them back.[6]

The totality of the chapter's narrative is here prefigured. All that will be added is the colouring. Brecht's scene-titles in *Mother Courage*, though rarely as full and often more provocative, signal his interest in the narrative techniques of the picaresque novel:

> Two years have passed. The war has spread far and wide. With scarcely a pause Mother Courage's little wagon rolls through Poland, Moravia, Bavaria, Italy, and back again to Bavaria. 1631. Tilly's victory at Magdeburg costs Mother Courage four officers' shirts. (Scene 5)

To be sure, the sacking of Magdeburg cost the lives of many and the livelihoods of all of its citizens. Within the ironically limited horizons of the picaresque, it is sufficient that Mother Courage lost four shirts. But there is, in these advertisements for Scene 5, a concealed explanation of the theatre's comparative neglect of the picaresque. As the demand for pictorial staging came to dominate theatres across Europe, questions of scenery intervened in the determination of subject-matter. Multiple settings and swift changes of location, simply accomplished on the page, may strain the credulity of an audience set in its ways of seeing. Brecht's play has sometimes (mistakenly) been performed in the grand style, as Mother Courage's Odyssey, but there is an assurance about Homer's epic that Brecht's assertively lacks. It is time, perhaps, to recognise in *Mother Courage* a rare masterpiece of picaresque drama, a dramaturgical relative of Ibsen's *Peer Gynt*, rather than seeking to relate it exclusively to the epic theatre, about which Brecht wrote so much.

The second German classic to inform *Mother Courage*, whether consciously or by silent assimilation, is the extraordinary first part of Friedrich Schiller's *Wallenstein* trilogy. *Das Lager* (*Wallenstein's Camp*) is, in fact, misrepresented by its traditional incorporation in a 'trilogy'. It is, rather, a one-act prologue, in which, before the beginning of a two-part tragedy about an Aristotelean hero, the military rank and file of the Thirty Years War are given a hearing. The setting prefigures *Mother Courage*: a canteen-tent with tables spread around it; soldiers at the tables, their children playing dice on a drum; mercenaries cooking on an open fire; the sound of singing from inside the tent; and the canteen-woman pouring wine. This canteen-woman, Gussie from Blasewitz in F. J. Lamport's resourceful translation, has one fatherless child to Mother Courage's three, but she also employs a nubile niece to attract and serve the soldiers and, like Mother Courage, she follows the war wherever it takes her. There is, however, a significant difference between Gussie and Mother Courage. In the overall design of Schiller's sequence of plays, the nature and the cost of loyalty are under scrutiny. Gussie is faithful to the Catholic cause. As she explains to her old friend, Lanky Peter from Itzehoe:

> To Temesoara and back again
> I followed with the baggage-train
> When we were harrying Mansfeld's heels.
> When Friedland laid siege to Stralsund, to his cost,
> I was there too – and my business was lost.
> I was with the relief of Mantua
> Came away with the Duke of Feria,
> And with a Spanish regiment
> On the way back I stopped at Ghent,
> Now in Bohemia my luck I'm trying.[7]

Perhaps, when Gussie's fortunes have sunk as low as Mother Courage's, she will purvey to Protestants and Catholics alike. But she has not yet come to Mother Courage's awareness of 'the purely mercantile character of war' (p. 393). She even offers drinks on the house when the soldiers resolve their differences in a chorus of loyalty to Wallenstein.

Although Schiller's attention is not focused on the financial underpinning of the Thirty Years War, he is not unaware of it. The common soldiers are attracted by the idea of their leader as a great man, but they are finally united by the recognition that Wallenstein has kept them better supplied than any other general. This is a mercenary army, encamped outside Pilsen. There are Irishmen, Walloons, Englishmen, Lombards, Swiss, Croats, Ulans and, of course, Bavarians. A typical soldier, like Lanky Peter, has already fought for the 'enemy' on occasions:

> When I served Gustavus, that miserable Swede!
> His camp was more like a chapel, indeed,
> Prayers every morning, straight after reveille,
> Each night at Lights Out, and before every sally;
> If we got a bit merry, like any good Germans,
> He was up on his horse and preaching us sermons.[8]

Compared with the interferingly godly Gustavus Adolphus, the Catholic commander-in-chief appeals to Lanky Peter as a liberator:

> For Tilly knew all about commanding.
> On himself he was strict and demanding,
> But the soldiers he would never cozen,
> And if he didn't have to foot the bill,
> His motto was: Live and let live! with a will.[9]

As one of the victorious army, Lanky Peter looks back with relish on the sacking of Magdeburg. Schiller's preliminary purpose is to explore the rift between the adherents of the Holy Roman Emperor and the adherents of Wallenstein through the eyes of the common soldier, and he carries it out in the roistering, deceptively doggerel rhymed verse that Goethe also deployed in *Faust*. These are Wallenstein's soldiers and, despite the ranting antagonism of a Capuchin friar, they come down on their general's side in the end. But even they realise that Wallenstein's officers are self-interested:

> They spent far more than they could earn,
> Thought it would bring them power in return.
> And they will be ruined one and all
> If the head that leads them, the Duke, should fall.

For Gussie, the issue is clear:

> Oh, God save me! That won't be funny!
> Half of the army owes me money.[10]

Mother Courage is cannier than Gussie.

Grimmelshausen and Schiller are literary and cultural ante-cedents of Brecht rather than direct sources for *Mother Courage*. Unlike Shakespeare, Brecht always adopted an oppositional stance towards his source-material. If the writing of this play came unusu-ally easily to him, that was primarily because he had long main-tained a view of war as a capitalist project, 'the continuation of business by other means' (p. 339). Two years before embarking on *Mother Courage*, he had been planning a play on Julius Caesar. By November 1937 he had read Plutarch, Suetonius and Theodor Mommsen's *History of Rome*, but, largely helpless in Danish libraries, he was seeking research assistance from a Paris-based acquaintance, Martin Domke. In a letter to Domke, Brecht outlines a possible scenario, much of which was later incorporated in the uncompleted novel, *The Business Affairs of Herr Julius Caesar*. The third act, for example, will be set in Gaul:

> According to Mommsen, the quantities of gold pouring in from Gaul caused a drop in the gold price. The war must be carried on with the utmost caution because of the requirements of the gold speculators. There must be a connection between this and the defeat at Aduatuca, where a whole region is lost.[11]

'How do I make the Gallic War a business?', he enquires of Domke. 'I need to know what sort of business was carried on between C. and the Gallic ruling class.' But the cynical exploitation of soldiers had been a theme of Brecht's writing since long before 1937. His poem 'The Legend of the Dead Soldier', written in 1918, had caused a scandal when he set it to music and sang it in a Berlin cabaret in 1921. There is nothing surprising about that. In a country still mourning its thousands of dead 'heroes', Brecht sang of a soldier who had displeased the Kaiser by dying before the war had been won and whose exhumed body, pronounced fit for active service, was shrouded in a German flag and marched back to battle. Before a publisher bold enough to print the poem could be found (1927), Brecht had seen staged the Darmstadt production of his anti-militaristic play *Man Is Man*. It was at about this time (September 1926) that he reached the conclusion that Karl Marx 'was the only spectator for my plays I'd ever come across'.[12] Galy Gay, the humble porter who is taken apart and re-assembled as a fighting-machine, vividly illustrates Marx's dictum that 'it is not the consciousness of men that determines their being, but on the contrary their social being determines their consciousness'.[13] The shift between the youthful anger of 'The Legend of the Dead Soldier' and the mature recognition of social conditioning as 'character' reflects Brecht's intensive reading of Marx during the early summer of 1926. To the exasperation of many critics and biographers, he was never again much interested in 'character', not even in his own.

Brecht set *Man Is Man* in a deliberately fictionalised British India, but its original audiences could not evade its reference to World War I. *Mother Courage*, whilst providing a kaleidoscopic retrospect on the Thirty Years War and World War I, has the future history of World War II in prospect. Brecht was intelligently aware that the Thirty Years War was an apter subject for dispassionate analysis than either of its twentieth-century counterparts. The German theatre, especially during its Expressionist phase, had been quicker to display its hatred of war than had the English-speaking theatre. Always gloomy about his likely reception in England, Brecht observed to his occasional collaborator Lion Feuchtwanger, 'evidently the English don't like nastiness as much as the Germans do'.[14] He would discover the same about the Americans. It is a contrast that can be well illustrated by brief reference to two plays, more or less contemporary with *Man Is Man*, that impressed audiences in their respective countries as definitively anti-war. *What Price Glory*, written by Maxwell Anderson and Laurence Stallings and staged in

New York in 1924, earned for its authors a reputation for gritty realism. Set in France during World War I, it shows a group of American marines as it could be reasonably assumed they 'really' were. Stallings, who had lost a leg in the war, had good cause not to romanticise American participation, but it is only the subject-matter that makes the play in any way exceptional. It is otherwise a conventional study of personalities in conflict. The same might be said of R. C. Sherriff's *Journey's End*, which startled London in 1928 with its depiction of panic in the front line of battle. Sherriff himself had been wounded in Flanders. Like Anderson and Stallings he was certainly set on de-glamourising war. There is no evidence in *Man Is Man* or in *Mother Courage* that Brecht had any such purpose. The possibility that there might be glamour in war seems simply not to have occurred to him. We cannot fairly assess the quality of *Mother Courage* if we remove the writing of it from its historical context. It is not merely an item in the ongoing catalogue of world drama; it is an attempt to intervene in world history. Brecht's amazing confidence that the rules governing human interaction, both nationally and internationally, can be changed survived even the anonymity and isolation of exile, but the letters and journals of the 1930s make it abundantly clear that the survival demanded an immense effort of will. 'These are ugly times', he wrote to Alfred Döblin in 1935, 'and you and I would have fitted so beautifully into the Age of Pericles.'[15]

Brecht's response to Nazi militarism was characteristically interrogative. He asked questions and placed his answers in the shared territory of logic and paradox. His model, as is made manifest in the *Messingkauf Dialogues*, was Socrates. Brecht's strategy, in *Mother Courage*, can be prefigured in a political question-and-answer session:

Question: Who profits from a war?
Answer: The profiteers.
Q: All the profiteers?
A: Some more than others.

Q: Where do the losers end up?

A: Dead.

Q: And the winners?

A: Dead, too. (What, after all, is the *real* difference between General Tilly's funeral and Kattrin's?)

Q: Who does the work to bring profit to the profiteers?

A: The soldiers.

Q: And what happens to the soldiers?

A: They starve. They get maimed or killed. Sometimes they eat.

Q: How do they eat?

A: Mother Courage sells them food at as high a price as she can get.

Q: Why does Mother Courage seek to exploit the soldiers?

A: Because she's a profiteer.

Q: But why exploit people of her own class?

A: Who else is there for her to exploit?

Q: But why exploit anyone?

A: Everyone exploits someone.

Q: Why?

A: The law of the market.

Q: So the big exploiters are copied by small exploiters who are copied by smaller exploiters?

A: And so *ad infinitum.*

Q: And the big exploiters are good for the national economy?

A: Very good.

Q: And the small exploiters?

A: Good, but not *very* good.

Q: And the smaller exploiters?

A: Better than nothing.

Q: And if there were only big exploiters?

A: People would begin to notice them.

Q: What then?

A: People might get angry.

Q: So, if Mother Courage stopped exploiting the soldiers . . . ?

A: Socialist revolution.

Q: I see – oh, and by the way, which is more important, a wagon or a child, my house or my children?

A: Ask your bank manager.

It is during a discussion of peace that the Chaplain asks his curious question, 'What becomes of the hole when the cheese has been eaten?' (p. 179). It is a riddle that supplies his argument that there is no need for war to end.

Mother Courage belongs, superficially at least, to a well-known dramatic species, the family-in-wartime play. Enduring war, the suffering family longs for peace and the chance to regroup. If Kattrin were allowed to dictate the terms, *Mother Courage* might have become a jewel in the crown of the (predominantly sentimental) family-in-wartime dramatic repertoire. But Brecht's Socratic contrariness leads him into subversion. Kattrin has maternal instincts but no prospect of children; her mother has children but no maternal instinct; there is a cook, but no food, a chaplain without a church and with minimal purchase on religion, and a paymaster (Swiss Cheese) who is innumerate. Given the rules by which Mother Courage conducts her life, it is always clear that peace will not harmonise this extended family. It is the rules that have to change.

Brecht wrote *Mother Courage* at the end of what was, for a follower of Marx, a peculiarly ugly decade. Not only had Fascism taken hold in Japan, Italy, Germany and Spain, but also the show-trials in Moscow inadequately disguised the descent of Soviet Communism into mass-murder. Stalin's deadly version of a 'new deal' gave an untimely fillip to what is, after all, the definitive enemy of Marxian Communism – cynicism. And cynicism, in its turn, nurtured the spirit of appeasement that enabled Hitler to convert a ruined nation into a vigorous war-machine.

In June 1940, while Lord Beaverbrook at the newly established Ministry of Aircraft Production was calling for a rapid increase in the output of British fighter-planes, Brecht was reflecting on the extent to which German rearmament in the 1930s had been 'the solution of the unemployment problem in the field of capitalism'.[16] While the Western democracies were feeling the effects of economic depression, there was full employment in Nazi Germany and the

Italian trains were running on time. The historian Eric Hobsbawm has recently categorised the period from 1914 to 1945 as 'the thirty-one years world war', and as 'an era of havoc comparable to the Thirty Years War'.[17] It was with such historical generalities that Brecht was preoccupied in the autumn of 1939, when he set about the composition of *Mother Courage*. He was anti-Nazi but never anti-German; nor did he deviate from the view that the mass of the people loses every war. The task he set himself was to write a play that would lay bare the reality of loss. Such a laying bare might enable the new audience, the audience of what he termed the scientific age, to perceive the interdependence of war and bourgeois hegemony. Much of the same territory that had been devastated by the imperial conflicts of the seventeenth century was under renewed threat from the imperial ambitions of Nazi Germany. By 1945 the devastation had been augmented by the victorious bourgeois democracies of the West. Returning to bomb-torn Berlin in 1948, Brecht saw the city as 'an etching by churchill after an idea by hitler'.[18] On 7 November 1939, four days after completing the first draft of *Mother Courage*, he had noted in his journal:

> the war displays a remarkably epic character, it teaches mankind about itself as it were, reads a lesson, a text to which the thunder of gunfire and the exploding bombs merely provide the accompaniment. it exposes its economic aims blatantly, in that it has direct recourse to economic means. conquests of markets provoke blockades in response, arms build-ups the withdrawal of raw materials. the ideological cover-up has worn so thin that it only serves to throw what is really happening into sharper relief.[19]

Brecht believed that, where catastrophe so vividly exposed contradiction, dialectics provided the only reliable aid to individual orientation. A bourgeois war might yet advance the proletariat: 'it is high time people began to derive dialectics from reality, instead of deriving it from the history of ideas, and using only selected examples from reality'.[20]

Brecht's name was not much known outside Germany when

Hitler's rise to power forced Brecht into exile. Ahead of him lay nearly fifteen years of constant endeavour to sustain, in the face of ignorance and neglect, his confidence in his own identity as a writer. The massive self-belief that antagonised many of the people who met him was his strongest ally. Even so, as he confided to his journal in September 1943, 'now and again I have a glimmering of the agonies of the untalented'.[21] This was written during the final (American) phase of his exile, when Hollywood seemed to offer the only market for his wares. Brecht often felt even more isolated in the English-speaking world than he had in Scandinavia. He made no English friends, and very few American, although his working relationship with Charles Laughton was a mutually fruitful one for a time. The isolation was, of course, exacerbated by the fact that America and Germany were at war, but that was by no means the whole story. The cultural milieu was alien to him, and he to it. Neither in Britain nor in America was there a theatre for his plays, and he lacked the capacity for graceful compromise. Respect for the audience did not mean, for Brecht, giving the public what it wanted. He wrote of and for a new audience, one that deserved the opportunity to learn. In America, his failure to accumulate wealth was generally read as evidence of his mediocrity. It is unlikely that he would have been better appreciated in Britain, where his lack of interest in military heroics would have aroused hostility. There was no precedent for *Mother Courage* in the English-speaking theatre. It was not a rooted concern for Pistol, Nym and Bardolph that drove Shakespeare to write *Henry V*. The play is inconceivable without the figure of the King himself, and it can hardly be doubted that Shakespeare reins back in the famous debate between the disguised King and the common soldiers who foresee their deaths in a quarrel not their own. This is not to deny Williams and Bates an honourable mention in a history of anti-war literature, but, like most common soldiers in fiction, they live in the shadow of their generals. This is not so in *Mother Courage*. No phrase more neatly encapsulates all that was anathema to Brecht than 'theirs not to reason why', but the phrase was and remains the basis of military discipline. It is not without significance that, in the year in which Brecht wrote *Mother Courage*, Penguin Books thought it worthwhile to reissue one of the earliest English novels with a World War I setting. To a reader in the 1990s, the bad faith of J. B. Morton's *The Barber of Putney* (1918) is palpable. Morton, a product of Harrow and Oxford who went on to earn a popular right-wing following as 'Beachcomber' in the *Daily Express*, centres his narrative on the unspectacular heroism of the British Tommy on the Western Front. It is an utter endorsement of the 'theirs not to reason why' approach to war: 'for the soldier in the trenches has no time to look beyond at the wider aspect. He does not see things in perspective. Talk of Paris and the Channel Ports and Amiens – well, after all, that was just more fighting. His business is simply with a few sandbags, a firestep, a fragment of trench.'[22] Morton's ignorance of the people about whom he writes is, however sentimentally camouflaged, an expression of unconscious contempt, but the object of his *conscious* contempt, voiced in the Introduction to a 1933 edition of *The Barber of Putney*, is very different. Brecht would certainly have fallen within the circle of Morton's fury:

> . . . during the past few years an exceptionally debased form
> of pacifism, growing out of the philosophy of materialism, has
> attempted to divide us into two camps: on one side ignorant, blood-
> thirsty militarists, and on the other, enlightened pacifists. It is the
> object of the self-styled enlightened people to persuade the young
> that the war was 'futile'; that those who fought were silly dupes, swept
> away by an emotional appeal; that nobody knew what it was about;
> that nobody can say who was guilty of beginning it all; and so on.
> The barber in my book went out to fight because it was his duty,
> and because he was too sane to sneer at the word 'honour'.[23]

This is the voice of the *Daily Express* bidding to become the voice of the people, but it fairly represents the dominant attitude (which, Brecht was wont to point out, is the attitude of the dominators) in Britain. It is scarcely surprising that *Mother Courage* was not performed there until 1955 nor in America until 1956.

Ten years divide the original writing of the play in Sweden

from its famous Berlin performance in 1949, but it was not Brecht's intention that the text should remain fixed and static. Without a theatre of his own, he was reduced to circulating manuscripts, knowing always that 'it is impossible to finish a play properly without a stage'.[24] It was, ideally, in rehearsal that he would select between variants and ensure that no information was being withheld from the audience. When eventually he worked with actors on *Mother Courage*, he recognised how the intervening years had detached the text from its original context and he made several changes. He had been unable to witness the play in performance at its world première in the Zürich Schauspielhaus on 19 April 1941. '[I]t is courageous of this theatre which is mainly composed of refugees to put on something of mine', he jotted in his Finland journal; 'no scandinavian stage had the guts to do it.'[25] It was hard for him to accept that no Scandinavian theatre had any particular reason to stage a play by a little-known German playwright, particularly one that made so few concessions to the prevailing taste. By contrast, Brecht's work was already familiar to several members of the Zürich company, to whom a production of *Mother Courage* signified an assertively German defiance of Hitler. The German-speaking American writer Thornton Wilder saw and admired the play there. Brecht would later invite him to translate *The Threepenny Opera*, which Wilder found superb, but too cool for him.[26] Attempts to peddle *Mother Courage* in America were no more successful. H. R. Hays published a translation in 1941, but failed to persuade anyone to produce it on the New York stage. In 1945, having found Laurette Taylor's playing of Amanda in Tennessee Williams's *The Glass Menagerie* 'epic', Brecht expressed a wish that she would play Mother Courage.[27] His contrary reaction on hearing that the soulful Eva Le Gallienne was interested in the part was a terse 'over my dead body',[28] but he made a personal approach to Elsa Lanchester, Charles Laughton's wife, who declined the part because she could not understand the play.[29] Brecht might have answered that the purpose of rehearsal is to make all things clear, but there is no evidence that he was given the chance to argue. At the time he was spending long hours with Laughton, working towards the production of *The Life of Galileo* that might yet establish his reputation in New York. What followed is, in its own way, part of the history of *Mother Courage*.

In one of the earliest American Gallup polls, whose results were announced in January 1939, a cross-section of citizens was asked which side, in the event of a war between Germany and the Soviet Union, it would wish to win. Eighty-three per cent opted for the Soviet Union.[30] The then-unpredicted effect of a victory over Germany, brought about in large measure by an alliance between the USA and the USSR, was an anti-communist hysteria which spread from Washington to Los Angeles and led to the shameful episode of the purging of Hollywood. Brecht was embroiled in the purge, as he early anticipated that he would be. It is clear in retrospect that the cold war had already begun before Jodl signed the instrument of unconditional surrender on 7 May 1945. It was made inevitable five days earlier, when the Red Army completed the capture of Berlin. The partition of Germany as a whole, and of Berlin in particular, has fundamentally affected the way in which Brecht is read. In simple terms, it has licensed an oppositional view of him as the proponent of an increasingly discredited political system. The truer view is of a playwright who, like Galileo, could not be relied on to take yes for an answer. It was under the supposition of a worldwide communist conspiracy that Brecht was called before the House Un-American Activities Committee on 30 October 1947. There is some irony in the timing, about ten weeks after the Los Angeles opening of the Brecht–Laughton *Galileo* and ten weeks before the due date for its transfer to New York. Brecht's own inquisition punctuated the two staged inquisitions of one of his finest creations. There was a price to pay. No longer secure in California, Brecht returned to Europe without a well-established plan of campaign. He would have gone anywhere to get his hands on a German-speaking theatre, always provided that the resident company was a serious one and the working conditions conducive to experiment; and it is at least possible that, but for the refusal of the State Department in Washington to issue him a visa, Brecht would have sought to establish his own company under the aegis of his old associate Erich Engel, now Intendant of the post-war Munich Kammerspiele. In the event, the crucial deal was struck with unenthusiastic Communist Party officials in East Berlin. They had first to reconcile themselves to the contrariness of Brecht's temperament and to his outspoken opposition to the official artistic policy of socialist realism, but when Wolfgang Langhoff, Intendant of the Deutsches Theater, invited Brecht to present one of his plays there, cautious approval was given. The agreed date for the opening was 11 January 1949. The play Brecht chose was *Mother Courage and Her Children*.

CHAPTER TWO

THE TEXT AND THE STAGE

The decision to write *Mother Courage* was taken shortly after the signing of the unlikely pact between Hitler's Germany and Stalin's Union of Socialist Republics. Brecht noted in his journal:

> the fact is that the russo-german pact makes the air clearer. what we have is a war between imperialist states. we have germany as the aggressor and warmonger. we have aggressive capitalism against defensive capitalism. the central powers need the war for conquest, the western powers need it to defend their conquests. there is enough barbarism to maintain a barbaric situation.[1]

This was the orthodox Marxist view at that time, and its impact on the writing of *Mother Courage* was decisive. Brecht depicts a war whose claims to be based on religious antagonism no longer fool anyone – except sometimes the Chaplain. The guiding light of the leaders is imperial conquest, and the promised reward the wealth of nations. It is Mother Courage's understanding of the war's priorities that licenses her heartless trade – the purveying of fodder to cannon-fodder. When the first production opened in Zürich in April 1941 the German army was completing its rapid conquest of Greece and the Balkan States, and Hitler, having failed in his attempt to bribe Molotov and Stalin with the promise of an eventual share in the British Empire, was impatiently planning the invasion of Russia. On 22 June 1941 that invasion, Hitler's Barbarossa campaign, was launched, and Winston Churchill broadcast his soon-to-be-broken promise:

> . . . we shall give whatever help we can to Russia and the Russian people. We shall appeal to all our friends and allies in every part

of the world to take this course and pursue it, as we shall, faithfully and steadfastly to the end.[2]

Nine days earlier, having crossed the Soviet Union by rail, Brecht had sailed from Vladivostok *en route* to California.

The outbreak of war between aggressive capitalism and (aggressive or defensive?) communism posed a threat to the premiss on which *Mother Courage* had originally been based – that the Thirty Years War, despite its claims to be based on genuine religious antagonism, was as much a battle between like and like as Hitler's war. But Brecht revised the text less than might have been expected. He had already recommended some emendations to the eleven-scene version used for the 1941 Zürich production, which lacked what appear as Scenes 7 and 10 in the most authoritative text. (Authoritative is a safer word than definitive.) For the second Zürich production in 1946 the play was reshaped into nine scenes, perhaps to clarify what Brecht called the 'curve of the dramaturgy'. The numbering, though, is deceptive. This was not an abridgement, as is clear from Brecht's brief annotations (pp. 331–3). In late 1948, when he came at last to work on a production himself, he found it important to make a few more changes, most significantly in Scenes 1 and 5, where attempts were made to obstruct any inclination in the audience to identify with Mother Courage. Some slight rethinking of the final scene after that production is reflected in the published text of the play (1950) which served as copy for Ralph Manheim's excellent translation (1972).

It may be that Brecht's reluctance to make major changes in the text of *Mother Courage*, even after Hitler's imperialist ambitions had brought the Red Army into the war, reveals his misgivings about the authenticity of Soviet communism. There was much detailed tinkering but no ideological reformation. There are sound historical reasons for that. With the German surrender imminent, Churchill wrote Stalin a personal letter which was not so much an example of his prescience as a commentary on the actuality of international relations at the time:

There is not much comfort in looking into a future where you and the countries you dominate plus the Communist parties in many other states are all drawn up on one side and those who rallied to the English-speaking nations and their associates or dominions are on the other. It is quite obvious that their quarrel would tear the world to pieces and all of us leading men on either side who had anything to do with that would be shamed before history. Even embarking on a long period of suspicion, of abuse and counter-abuse, and of opposing policies would be a disaster hampering the great development of world prosperity for the masses which is attainable only by our trinity.[3]

Since Franklin Roosevelt had died two weeks earlier, the trinity of leading men who would be 'shamed before history' now consisted, in Churchill's mind, of himself, Stalin and Harry S Truman, whose equivalents in the Thirty Years War are not difficult to find. Brecht had his own views about history's leading men, as well as a more active concern for 'world prosperity for the masses' than either Stalin or Britain's rhetorical Prime Minister. The Europe to which he had newly returned was a continent that not only looked back on a recent war but also had cause to fear the outbreak of another one. Small wonder, then, that Brecht felt confident of the abiding relevance of *Mother Courage*. Within a week of his arrival in Zürich he was helping to draft a proclamation in the name of writers all over the world:

The expectation of another war paralyses the reconstruction of the world. Today, the choice we face is no longer between peace and war, but peace or destruction. To those politicians who still do not understand this fact, we state emphatically that the peoples want peace.[4]

More specifically, the proclamation drew attention to the fact that 'the existence of two different economic systems in Europe is being exploited for a new war propaganda'. It was in Berlin that the conflicting economic systems were most visibly and constantly in friction during the cold war. While the capitalist West of the city showily reaped the benefits of the Marshall Plan after June 1947, the communist East struggled with the after-effects of the ruined harvest of 1946 and the savage winter of 1946–7. American economic aid was capitalism's bright shop-window, but it concealed a paranoia that, in the years between 1947 and the building of the Berlin Wall in 1961, carried the minute-by-minute threat of yet another European conflagration. In 1948 the Americans prepared contingency plans for military intervention in Italy, should the Communists win the election there. In 1950, by taking up arms in Korea, the West proved that its threats were not idle. In the intervening year Brecht staged *Mother Courage* in Berlin, thereby putting the finishing touch to a play written as one war started, and staged, as he must often have thought, on the eve of another.

It is unwise to read a play by Brecht without reference to his intentions for its staging. The conformation of actors on the platform, the gestic significance of their grouping, was in his mind as he wrote. Rehearsal provided an opportunity to interrogate the text, never to polish performance to the point where it rendered the text inconspicuous. Always conscious that human beings cease to notice whatever they take for granted, Brecht sought out the theatrical means to elucidate what is astonishing in the commonplace, to show that the given circumstances of our living are neither necessary nor even likely. They have been created, historically and materially, and can therefore be changed. It is because Brecht's writing is so intrinsically linked to performance that my analysis of *Mother Courage* will make frequent reference to the details of Brecht's own production of the play, details which are readily available in the published Model Book and in major translations of the play (pp. 334–86).

SCENE I

At the play's opening the stage is bare, save for two shivering soldiers. They are on an evidently futile recruiting mission, seeking out new troops for the army of the Swedish General Oxenstjerna. Typically, it is not the General whom we see. The real work of war is done by small men. Brecht's commentary in the Model Book characteristically details the narrative steps of the scene in a sequence of discrete sentences, thus underlining a principle of epic construction – 'one thing after another' rather than 'one thing out of another'. It is important, if we are to avoid the trap of taking the narrative for granted, that each element in it should be separately noticeable. If the incidents flow too smoothly from and into each other they are liable to appear inevitable. This is Brecht's account:

> Recruiters are going about the country looking for cannon fodder. Mother Courage introduces her mixed family, acquired in various theatres of war, to a sergeant. The canteen woman defends her sons against the recruiters with a knife. She sees that her sons are listening to the recruiters and predicts that the sergeant will meet an early death. To make her children afraid of the war, she has them too draw black crosses. Because of a small business deal, she nevertheless loses her brave son. And the sergeant leaves her with a prophecy:
>
> 'If you want the war to work for you
> You've got to give the war its due'. (*p. 342*)

The opening dialogue between Recruiter and Sergeant is immediately about war. The Sergeant is a military professional with a habit of mouthing what would be homespun philosophy if it were not so jarringly paradoxical. That is to say that the actor is invited to pronounce, as if they were truisms, several shocking views of war. There is an immediate disjunction between the things said and the manner in which they are said: 'How can you have morality without a war?'; 'In peacetime the human race goes to the dogs'; 'Like all good things, a war is hard to get started.' Such apparent paradoxes are, of course, distinct from lies:

> I've been in places where they hadn't had a war in as much as seventy years, the people had no names, they didn't even know who they were. It takes a war before you get decent lists and records.

The Recruiter is more intent on his impossible task – to recruit four whole platoons in a sparsely populated back-of-beyond. It is he who spots the approaching wagon, in which Mother Courage makes her utterly astonishing entrance. Harnessed like horses (the horse is already a casualty of war), Eilif and Swiss Cheese are pulling the covered wagon at the front of which their mother and sister sit. The wagon is a mobile home, not yet anything more. As it changes form and appearance over the remaining scenes it will assume a personality of its own, a fourth child almost for Mother Courage. The entrance, as so often in the kind of melodrama which this play certainly is not, is announced by music – Kattrin playing a Jew's harp. It is simultaneously a theatrical joke and one of the interruptions of an action which serve as alienating devices (*Verfremdungseffekte*) in Brecht's theatre. But the dislocation does not end there. Having answered the Sergeant's question, 'Who are you?', with a curt 'Business people', Mother Courage sings a two-stanza advertising song with the raucous refrain:

> The spring is come. Christian, revive!
> The snowdrifts melt. The dead lie dead.
> And if by chance you're still alive
> It's time to rise and shake a leg.

Within a few minutes of its opening, *Mother Courage* has several times forced us to wonder just what kind of a play it is.

We know the historical period in which it is set, and we quickly learn that we are with the Protestant army of Gustavus Adolphus. Mother Courage is on her way to the camp of the Second Finnish Regiment. War is as much her business as it is the Sergeant's. Her three children, variously acquired, bear witness to a variety of smaller wars that preceded this big one. She is from Bamberg in Bavaria, but her family is pan-European. Eilif's surname is Nojocki (at the end of Scene 2 she calls him a 'Finnish devil') because 'his father always claimed to be called Kojocki or Mojocki'. Swiss Cheese's father was Swiss, but his surname is Frejos because 'when he came I was with a Hungarian'. Kattrin, surnamed Haupt, is half German. Brecht makes no attempt to create complex characters for them. It is sufficient that Eilif is brave, Swiss Cheese honest and Kattrin compassionate, since those are the traits that are going to kill them. Bravery, honesty and compassion are not, of course, simple qualities, and the children's possession of them is subject to the audience's questioning. Whenever Brecht employs abstractions he opens them to our scrutiny. Mother Courage, for example, owes her own nickname to the fact that 'when I saw ruin staring me in the face I drove out of Riga through cannon fire with fifty loaves of bread in my wagon'. Courage, as conventionally understood, was not a quality Brecht admired: parachutists, he wrote in his journal, 'are dropped like bombs, and bombs do not need courage. the thing that would take courage would be to refuse to climb into the plane in the first place.'[5] Where her trade is concerned (and when is it not?) Mother Courage's courage is that of the parachutist, and Brecht does not intend us to admire it. Nor, in the course of the play, does she learn any better. The courage that carried her out of Riga is still present in the retreating, lone figure at the end of the final scene.

Brecht identifies the pivotal point of Scene 1 as the moment when, having assessed the physique of the two boys, for all the world like a racehorse owner about to make a purchase, the Sergeant crosses the stage to Mother Courage, comes to a standstill in front of her and asks, 'Why aren't they in the army?' It marks the beginning of serious bartering, after which Mother Courage's eagerness to sell a buckle has cost her her elder son. During the course of rehearsal Helene Weigel developed a distinctive mannerism of audibly snapping shut the leather money-bag slung from her neck. Such details, Brecht explains, were worked out 'painstakingly and inventively in accordance with the principle of epic theatre: *one thing after another*'. There is much to be inferred about the practice of the Berliner Ensemble from the associated recommendation that 'the pace at rehearsals should be slow, if only to make it possible to work out details; determining the pace of the performance is another matter and comes later' (p. 346). Brecht's written text reveals an equal alertness to the telling detail, often with a humorous or ironic sting in its tail. An example in Scene 1 is Mother Courage's response to the Sergeant's request for her papers. She digs out of a tin box a certificate confirming that her (dead) horse is free of foot-and-mouth disease, a map of Moravia and a missal. Mother Courage is obviously confident enough that religion is of no great significance in this 'religious' war. She would not otherwise risk presenting to Protestant soldiers a Catholic book of devotion, even one she claims to have picked up to wrap cucumbers in. Brecht finds it difficult to resist the temptation to make sport with the hypocritical posturings of warring Christians. The Recruiter will later reassure Eilif: 'it's been said to our discredit that a lot of religion goes on in the Swedish camp . . . that's slander to blacken our reputation. Hymn singing only on Sunday, one verse! And only if you've got a voice.'

SCENE 2

Even without prior knowledge of Brecht's slipperiness, the audience should be aware, by the end of Scene 1, that this is a play that handles reasonably familiar dramatic material in an unconventional way. A confessed con woman whose name features in the title has been conned, but, instead of carrying a resolution to be revenged on the whole pack of them, she has walked off beside her wagon with the modesty of a minor character. One episode is over. For all we know the next one may have nothing in particular to do with it. Two years have passed, and Mother Courage is still with the Swedish army. Brecht's sentence-by-sentence account of Scene 2 again records the way in which it was broken down during rehearsals:

> Mother Courage sells provisions at exorbitant prices in the Swedish camp; while driving a hard bargain over a capon, she makes the

acquaintance of an army cook who is to play an important part in her life. The Swedish general brings a young soldier into his tent and honours him for his bravery. Mother Courage recognizes her lost son in the young soldier; taking advantage of the meal in Eilif's honour, she gets a steep price for her capon. Eilif relates his heroic deed, and Mother Courage, while plucking her capon in the kitchen adjoining the tent, expresses opinions about rotten generals. Eilif does a sword dance and his mother answers with a song. Eilif hugs his mother and gets a slap in the face for putting himself in danger with his heroism. (*p. 348*)

If this scene is to be accurately played, the disposition of the stage must be carefully considered. There is no call for the wagon, but there is a danger, so early in the play, that its absence will be inconspicuous. Anyone working on a production should be prepared, on issues like this, to consult the Model Book. This is one of many Brechtian scenes of split action. Although the actors in one part of the stage may show their ignorance of the antics of those in another part, in effect they will be commentating on those antics. In Scene 1, in a stage-image that invites speculations on mother-love, the price of masculinity and the egotism of survival, the Recruiter, concealed from Mother Courage and the Sergeant by the wagon, buys Eilif moments before the Sergeant buys a buckle. In Scene 2, while her bought son obliviously revels, Mother Courage exploits his short-lived success to raise the price of her capon. Split action of this kind must be precisely timed. There are capons on both parts of the stage.

Brecht's pleasure in learning about his own plays in rehearsal is often recorded in his subsequent observations. Working with Helene Weigel and Paul Bildt on Scene 2 sharpened his awareness of the ease with which the mutual respect of the Cook and Mother Courage tipped towards fondness:

> Both showed pleasure in the bargaining, and the cook expressed his admiration not only for her ready tongue but also for the shrewdness with which she exploited the honouring of her son for business

purposes. Courage in turn was amused at the way the cook fished the chunk of rotten beef out of the garbage barrel with the tip of his long meat knife and carried it, carefully as though it were a precious object – though to be kept at a safe distance from one's nose – over to his kitchen table. (*p. 350*)

The Cook's rescuing of the beef is the visible sign that Mother Courage's attempt at extortion has failed. It is the lucky chance of Eilif's arrival that turns the tables in her favour. Because of her capacity to survive, readers of the play – and sometimes even audiences – come away with the impression that Mother Courage is habitually a winner. In fact, this is the only occasion on which she unambiguously gets the better of a bargain. It is in the relationship of Cook and Canteen-Woman that the 'business idyll' of which Brecht writes is fitfully glimpsed through the play. For a short while, in Scene 9, the idyll will promise to find a permanent home in an inn in Utrecht.

The Chaplain's entry into the play is altogether less auspicious. The General, whilst indulging Eilif, treats the Chaplain like a skivvy, thus revealing, as Brecht mischievously observes, 'the role of religion in a war of religion' (p. 350). Disregarded in his first scene, the Chaplain remains, despite his occasional fits of self-assertion, a minor force throughout the play. Soldiers have traditionally held non-combatants in low regard, and this Chaplain is no businessman either. Not knowing how to exploit the war, he tries to do his best by it and is rewarded by contempt on all sides. Despite the fact that his is the second largest speaking part in the play, he remains curiously in abeyance throughout. Brecht has some fun with him, as he does with almost all military personnel in his plays. Armies take themselves terribly seriously, and this invites mockery. When he heard, in 1942, that the American army was using hormone injections to eliminate traces of homosexuality in soldiers, Brecht's response was, 'so the army isn't any fun even for homosexuals any more'.[6] The Swedish General whom Eilif enraptures may be one of the lucky ones who still has his fun. Brecht is sly about the General's sexuality.

His production notes, in overt contradiction of the text, propose that the attention paid to Eilif is 'a matter of routine action', performed 'almost absently' (p. 350). In his own Berlin production, he felt that they got the General wrong – too much a rowdy drunk, too little the effete Swedish aristocrat, representative of a class that has long taken everything for granted. It was not yet easy, in 1949, to present homosexuality on stage, and there may have been some evasiveness in the actor's exhibition of drunkenness.

An army is employed to maintain the power-base of those in authority, and the individual soldier is therefore fighting to maintain the conditions of his own subjection. It would be difficult to argue for the adequacy of Brecht's post-war formulation that 'the war must be described as the german bourgeoisie's war which they commissioned hitler to manage',[7] but its consistency is not in dispute. The cautionary tale of Eilif is implicitly an invitation to the proletariat, not so much to think again as to think. Eilif's bravery never rises much above the level of bullying. In Scene 2 Mother Courage claims that he is intelligent as well as brave – and, in comparison with Swiss Cheese, perhaps he is – but the purloining of the ox, the act of war for which he is here exalted, exhibits little more than the cunning of a street-fighter when threatened with a citizen's arrest. He is a uniformed mugger, licensed by war to round off robbery with murder, and it is evidence of Mother Courage's limited understanding that she cannot entirely suppress her pride in him. To be sure she slaps his face 'for not surrendering when the four of them were threatening to make hash out of you', but the assault is an ambiguous one. She cannot develop her insight that only a poor general needs brave soldiers into a recognition that Eilif's collaboration in an imperialist war is a betrayal of his own interests. If she could, the play of *Mother Courage* would end here, or another play – something closer to Brecht's stage version of Gorky's *The Mother* – begin. As it is, the centrepiece of the scene, Eilif's song-and-dance act, is a piece of grotesque triumphalism which cannot be cancelled out by Mother Courage's deflationary coda.

SCENE 3

Scene 3 is much the longest in the play, which is almost half over when it ends. As ever, the position of the wagon is a crucial determinant of the on-stage action. In Berlin it was placed not too far stageright to cramp the groupings to the right of it. Importantly, those who took up position there could not see or be seen by anyone elsewhere on the stage. Brecht is insistent that the rhythms should be carefully established:

> In scene 3 a camp idyll is disrupted by the enemy's surprise attack. The idyll should be composed from the start in such a way as to make it possible to show a maximum of disruption. It must leave room for people to run back and forth in clearly laid-out confusion; the parts of the stage must be able to change their functions. (*p. 354*)

Three years have passed and Mother Courage is still doing business with the Swedish army. There is a lull in the war. Brecht breaks the scene down as follows:

> Black marketing in ammunition. Mother Courage serves a camp whore and warns her daughter not to take up with soldiers. While Courage flirts with the cook and the chaplain, mute Kattrin tries on the whore's hat and shoes. The surprise attack. First meal in the Catholic camp. Conversation between brother and sister and arrest of Swiss Cheese. Mother Courage mortgages her wagon to the camp whore in order to ransom Swiss Cheese. Courage haggles over the amount of the bribe. She haggles too long and hears the volley that lays Swiss Cheese low. Mute Kattrin stands beside her mother to wait for the dead Swiss Cheese. For fear of giving herself away, Courage denies her dead son. (*pp. 351–2*)

The aim of rehearsal, in other words, was to learn to play the sequences one after another, each sequence being mined for its own meanings. At the opening of the scene, Mother Courage and Kattrin are folding washing. Brecht's note is of significance to the play as a whole: 'Courage's unflagging readiness to work is important. She is

Plate 1 Teo Otto's designs for productions of *Mother Courage* – this one for a 1952 staging by the Compagnia del Teatro dei Satiri in Rome – always precisely place the wagon for each scene.

hardly ever seen not working. It is her energy and competence that make her lack of success so shattering' (p. 355). Two visual signs indicate the present state of business and the present state of the war: the wagon is well stocked and the cannon is serving as a clothes-prop. A weapon of destruction has been commandeered – and 'made strange' – for domestic purposes. Mother Courage does not interrupt her linen-folding in order to haggle with the ordnance officer over the price of black-market bullets. The sequence is an echo in performance of an acting exercise Brecht commended: two participants continue to fold linen whilst feigning a violent quarrel. The intended effect is to draw attention to the strangeness of activities which might otherwise be taken for granted. The corruptness of the bargain is as odd, and yet as matter-of-fact and unexceptional, as household washing, and Mother Courage sees no inconsistency in following her crooked deal with an admonition to Swiss Cheese to be honest. Equally, she sees no incongruity in laundering clothes for people, Swiss Cheese among them, who may be dead before they have a chance to wear them. The war, she reports, is 'getting along pretty well', and 'more countries are joining in all the time' (most of them rather as Ethiopia 'joined in' when Mussolini invaded in 1935).

There follows one of the three-character sequences of which the play is unusually full. The Berlin arrangement was for Mother Courage to carry her sewing downstage and sit with Yvette whilst Kattrin continued to remove washing from the makeshift line. Kattrin's eyes and ears are trained on the downstage pair. The triangle is an active one, not least because Mother Courage, whilst speaking with Yvette, is pointing the moral of Yvette's fate at her upstage daughter. If Kattrin did not already have erotic fantasies, the attempt to divert her from them would probably create them in her. Such protectiveness in parents is generally a provocation. Yvette, already suffering from a venereal disease, sips brandy as she tells the sad tale of her downfall. The story of Pete the Pipe and the ruined maid is one of a number of insets in the play. Were it not for Brecht's refusal to handle it as such, it would be the most Aristotelean. Already clued in to the identity of Yvette's seducer if the Cook has smoked his pipe in Scene 2, the audience will be confident of it when he lights up a little later in Scene 3; but Brecht delays the recognition (Aristotle's term was *anagnorisis*) until Scene 8, by which time Yvette's war-worn vindictiveness has no dramatic relevance. For the moment, Kattrin works and listens to the story of Yvette's first sexual adventure. It is true enough that there is nothing complex about Kattrin's character, but that does not mean that it is easy to know how to play her. Nor is Brecht an entirely reliable guide. 'It is necessary', he writes, 'to show an intelligent Kattrin from the start. (Her infirmity misleads actors into representing her as dull.)' But is it necessary? The text does not demand that it should be so. At this point in the Model Book Brecht is concerned to make a point: 'it is the war that breaks her, not her infirmity; in technical terms, the war must find something that remains to be broken' (p. 365). Kattrin may not be a moron, but she is severely traumatised from the start: 'a soldier stuffed something in her mouth when she was little'. Brecht's primary purpose here may be to provoke doubt, to deter actor and director from taking things for granted. The effect of rehearsal on a text is well exemplified in the next episode of Scene 3. Brecht's descriptive sentence links physically separated actors: 'While Courage flirts with the cook and chaplain, mute Kattrin tries on the whore's hat and shoes.' This is not quite what happened in the Berlin production. The sexual banter that follows Yvette's drunken exit and the entrance of Chaplain and Cook begins on the open stage, but after the Chaplain's randy reference to Kattrin as 'this delightful young lady' Mother Courage leads her guests behind the wagon – out of harm's way. If the conversation that continues there is a flirtation, it is only so because Mother Courage is as combative in sexual commerce as she is in commerce in general. The dialogue of the Cook and Mother Courage contains some of the play's most telling observations on war. Brecht did not want the audience distracted by Kattrin's pantomime. There was, therefore, an interpolation, unrecorded in the published text. Yvette's story, together with the attentions of the Cook and Chaplain, has set Kattrin's imagination racing. While Mother Courage serves brandy behind the wagon, Kattrin moves downstage, her eyes fixed on the hat and the boots. Mother Courage has meanwhile made her verbal assault on the Poles for 'butting into their own affairs' when Gustavus Adolphus was marching his army over their land, and the Chaplain has backed her up with a party-line celebration of Gustavus, the liberator of enslaved races. It is at this point in the published text that the Cook delivers his long revisionist speech about the Swedish King. In the Berlin performance, though, he broke off after the first sentence to lead a rendition of the Lutheran hymn 'Ein' feste Burg ist unser Gott.' According to Brecht, they sang it 'with feeling', but looking round anxiously, 'as though such a song were illegal within the Swedish camp' (p. 357). It was during the singing that Kattrin tried on the hat and boots. A sequence of photographs in the Model Book shows Angelika

Hurwicz as Kattrin, skirt hoisted and hat jammed on to her head, testing and admiring the boots which comically fail to transform her. As the hymn ends, her feverish movements end with it, and the Cook resumes, 'But we were talking about the king . . . ' What he has to say might well pass for treason in the Swedish camp. It is a clever but straightforward debunking of Protestant myth-making, but Mother Courage's response is among the finest examples of Brechtian slyness. 'He can't be defeated because his men believe in him', she says, and continues *earnestly* (the adverb is a masterstroke in its own right):

> When you listen to the big wheels talk, they're making war for reasons
> of piety, in the name of everything that's fine and noble. But when
> you take another look, you see that they're not so dumb; they're
> making war for profit. If they weren't, the small fry like me wouldn't
> have anything to do with it.

'That's a fact', says the Cook as Kattrin begins her inept imitation of a whorish strut. Behind the wagon Mother Courage affirms that 'We're all good Protestants here! Prosit!' She lifts her glass, and the Catholic attack begins.

When he encountered his own text in the rehearsal room Brecht did not confine himself to the theatrical interpretation of given material. The text was something for the rehearsing actors to think about. Its effective mediation was a matter of general interest, a subject for discussion. The outcome of such discussion, as in the sequence considered above, might be a re-visioning; but it was of particular importance at all times that the actors should have their own opinions. Weigel, whilst speaking Mother Courage's lines, might not agree with them. So much the better: if the disagreement is implicit in the performance, the audience can benefit from the dialectical tension between actor and character. The attitude is one of enquiry. How, for example, are the actors to sing 'Ein' feste Burg'? The answer provided by Brecht's note is not so much an answer as an invitation to ask more questions. If they sing it with feeling, is the

Plate 2 Brecht and Helene Weigel in one of the discussions that
characterised Brecht's rehearsals for the 1949 production.

feeling the same for all of them? For the Chaplain as well as the Cook? And why does the singing of so politically correct a hymn make them nervous? Are they all nervous in the same way? And what is the effect of turning the hymn into a musical accompaniment to an early exercise in a prostitute's training programme?

Although he is the least voluble of the brandy-drinkers, the Chaplain is already a focus of attention before the Catholic raid. Religion is, after all, his trade, and he might be expected to contribute when it is the topic of debate. But the surprise attack transforms his life as well as his costume. Amid the frenzied on-stage action he is a fixed point, standing still and obstructing everyone. He has become a displaced person, a refugee, and the interpretation of his behaviour during what remains of Scene 3 constitutes a Brechtian crux that anticipates the more frequently acknowledged crux of Kattrin's death in Scene 11. It is clear enough that Brecht mistrusted emotion, in himself as well as in the theatre – and there are historical reasons for that. In the plays that he deplored, and in the actors and audiences whom he hoped to change, he recognised a tendency for feeling to overwhelm thought rather than to co-exist with it. Such supervention operated as a block on the scrutiny of causes, which was the project he had set himself. But it is ludicrous to present Brecht as a playwright who avoided emotionally load-bearing scenes. Grusha's story in *The Caucasian Chalk Circle* is a composite of them. So is *The Life of Galileo*. It would be truer to say that Brecht is among the theatre's most consummate craftsmen of the searing episode. What he introduced to such episodes was an awareness of the contradictions they contained and the social realities they exposed. Quite often, as in the example of an 'intelligent' Kattrin, he deliberately complicated in discussion aspects of his plays whose contradictoriness might otherwise be overlooked. So it is with the Chaplain. How are we to reconcile his singing of the lyrical *Horenlied* with Brecht's statement that 'he shows no exaggerated involvement in the tragedy of the honest son' (p. 358)? In the 1949 production, uncharacteristically, the issue was ducked. The

Horenlied was not sung because its purposes could not be negotiated in rehearsal. Early in the process, Brecht had recorded his approval of the way in which Hinz 'does the atheist chaplain as if he had lost his faith much as some other poor devil might have lost his leg'.[8] But to declare the Chaplain an atheist is to over-determine his case. When Erwin Geschonneck took over the part for the 1951 revival, the *Horenlied* was restored. Its proleptic relating of Swiss Cheese's suffering with Christ's Passion surely indicates the Chaplain's involvement in 'the tragedy of the honest son'.

Such involvement has its perils for both actor and audience. It was Brecht's custom to ask of human charity (*Menschlichkeit*) that it should do something more than preserve the status quo. The Young Comrade of *The Measures Taken* was guilty of an overwhelming impulse to alleviate suffering when his set task was to eliminate its causes. In contrast, the Chaplain's charity is entirely passive. As so often, Brecht raises the question 'What good is goodness?' It might be argued that, even on a level of homespun morality – of 'leaving the place better than you found it' – the Chaplain is doomed to ineffectiveness. But this is to make the play sound cooler than it is. *Mother Courage* is punctuated with warm exchanges, none more poignant than the Scene 3 'conversation' between Swiss Cheese and Kattrin, about which Brecht provides an informative note:

> The short conversation between mute Kattrin and Swiss Cheese is quiet and not without tenderness. Shortly before the destruction we are shown for the last time what is to be destroyed. The scene goes back to an old Japanese play in which two boys conclude a friendship pact. Their way of doing this is that one shows the other a flying bird, while the second shows the first a cloud. (*p. 358*)

Equally indicative of Brecht's interest in human/humane detail is a reference to Geschonneck's 'extraordinarily gentle, embarrassed gesture' of protest when Mother Courage tells Kattrin not to howl like a dog because it gives the Chaplain the creeps.[9]

The last half of Scene 3 is dominated by the pursuit and

execution of Swiss Cheese. Parallels with Christ's Passion are not confined to the *Horenlied*: 'This is the third day', Swiss Cheese reminds us shortly after the mid-scene break; Mother Courage denies her son three times; Yvette, a note in the Model Book suggests, gives Mother Courage 'the kiss of Judas' as she schemes to take her wagon; and the silent scream, Helene Weigel's most famous single gesture, with which Mother Courage greets the off-stage volley that signals her son's death, recalls the moment of terror when the veil of the Temple was rent in twain. The effect of the superficially incongruous linking of Swiss Cheese's death and Christ's Passion is not deflationary. On the one hand, it makes the Crucifixion as matter-of-fact as a minor military execution outside a nameless village; on the other it heightens our perception of Swiss Cheese as a sacrificial victim. That is to say that the audience must choose whether or not to evade the inference that Christ's death was, politically speaking, as ineffective as Swiss Cheese's. The wonder, perhaps, is not that Brecht initially agreed to omit the *Horenlied* but that he had the nerve to restore it.

The silent scream embodies a rare moment of recognition on the part of Mother Courage. She has haggled too long and too often, and as a result her honest son is dead. A superb sequence of archival photographs preserves this extraordinary stage-moment. Weigel is sitting to the left of the barrel-table and Geschonneck to the right. Four-square to the audience and almost moronically bewildered, he is drying glasses. In the first photograph Weigel is leaning forward, mouth wide open, hands scrabbling at the lap of her skirt. In the second she has thrown her head back as if baying silently to the moon. Her fingers are still tense. Geschonneck wears the puzzled look of a schoolmaster who has just sat on a drawing-pin. In the third Weigel holds the same position, although her fingers are beginning to relax. Geschonneck has gone. Another photograph, not in the sequence, shows him lumbering helplessly towards the wagon. The final picture is of Weigel steadying herself for the next crisis. Her hands lie loose in her lap, her body is slightly hunched, her eyes are closed, and her bottom lip pouts sullenly from a down-turned mouth. It is with an expression not unlike this that she will deny knowledge of the corpse's identity:

> When the soldiers come in with the dead boy and she is asked to look at him, she stands up, goes over, looks at him, shakes her head, goes back and sits down. During all this she has an obstinate expression, her lower lip thrust forward. Here Weigel's recklessness in throwing away her character reaches its highest point. (*p. 360*)

Brecht admired Weigel's willingness to repel the audience's sympathy. He admired, also, her powers of observation, recall and alteration:

> Her look of extreme suffering after she has heard the shots, her unscreaming open mouth and backward-bent head probably derived from a press photograph of an Indian woman crouched over the dead body of her son during the shelling of Singapore. Weigel must have seen it years before, though when questioned she did not remember it. That is how observations are stored up by actors. Actually it was only in the later performances that Weigel assumed this attitude. (*p. 360*)

Swiss Cheese's fate reinforces a recognition that, though the family may complicate trade for Mother Courage, it cannot negate it. Hers is the necessary egotism of the underclass. In the end she cannot support more than one person – herself.

SCENE 4

This short scene is a very bold piece of writing. In the pictorial theatre it might well have been set in front of the curtain to allow a change of scenery behind. But that is not Brecht's purpose. After the emotional climax of Scene 3 he confronts the audience with a startling change of mood. As a result of the Catholic incursion Mother Courage has lost a son. We might expect her to mourn, but she decides to register a complaint. The Catholics have ripped up her wagon and she wants compensation. It is scarcely credible that she believes she will get it; but, then, this is a scene in which art attempts to come to terms, not with real life, but with reality. It is an illustrative inset, dominated theatrically by 'The Song of the Great Capitulation'. Brecht analyses its progress as follows:

> Mother Courage is sitting outside the captain's tent; she has come to put in a complaint about damage to her wagon; a clerk advises her in vain to let well enough alone. A young soldier appears, also to make a complaint; she dissuades him. The bitter 'Song of the Great Capitulation'. Courage herself learns from the lesson she has given the young soldier and leaves without having put in her complaint. (*pp. 360–1*)

It is through observing the Young Soldier that Mother Courage comes to her resolution. He is angry enough to enter the tent of a Catholic captain shouting obscenities about the Virgin Mary. His anger may even be justified. But the crucial question, posed to him by Mother Courage, is 'How long won't you put up with injustice?' The only anger that can help the people is the anger that lasts long enough to change the world order. Brecht provides a provocatively slippery note:

> In no other scene is Courage as depraved as in this one . . .
> Nevertheless Weigel's face in this scene shows a glimmer of wisdom and even of nobility, and that is good. Because the depravity is not so much that of her person as that of her class, and because she herself at least rises above it somewhat by showing that she understands this weakness and that it even makes her angry. (*pp. 361–2*)

This is a scene that is almost certain to trouble actors and directors who depend on psychological cues for action. Its greater purpose is sharply articulated by Robert Leach:

> Because both complainers in the scene decide against carrying their complaints through, we should not imagine that Brecht is saying, 'Don't bother to complain, don't rock the boat'. What he is saying is, 'Be aware of what complaining involves' and 'How can complaining change things?'. He is interested in directing our attention towards ways of complaining which will be effective.[10]

SCENE 5

In Scene 5 we encounter for the first time a significant event in the Thirty Years War. The sacking of Magdeburg by Tilly's triumphant Catholic army was a previously unparalleled atrocity, and a playwright of pacifist inclinations might have been expected to make much of it. Brecht does no such thing, as the laconic final sentence of the scene-title has already implied: 'Tilly's victory at Magdeburg costs Mother Courage four officers' shirts.' This may be a famous foreign field, but we are confined to some corner of it. The phrasing of the scene in rehearsal was as follows:

> After a battle. Courage refuses to give the chaplain her officers' shirts to bandage wounded peasants with. Kattrin threatens her mother. At the risk of her life Kattrin saves an infant. Courage laments the loss of her shirts and snatches a stolen coat away from a soldier who has stolen some schnapps, while Kattrin rocks the baby in her arms.
> (p. 362)

'I've got to think of myself', says Mother Courage at the height of her confrontation with Kattrin. She is, of course, right. If she is to survive, let alone thrive, the small-time trader must emulate the ruthlessness of the multinational company. The big profit at Auschwitz went to I. G. Farben for supplying the ovens, but Mother Courage might have been there, selling faulty gas-masks along a queue of Jews.

There was a significant difference in the staging of Scene 5 for the Zürich première. There, grumbling all the way, Therese Giehse as Mother Courage took it upon herself to rip the shirts. The Berlin restaging was designed to deny the audience a sympathetic glimpse of motherhood overwhelming commercial considerations. Brecht was always aware that the play invited an audience's admiration for the vitality of an indomitable woman. In rehearsal he was more concerned to contradict such an interpretation than to prevent it. Contradiction was his natural mode of dramatic and political discourse. It implies a constant dialogue with the audience. Thus, in Scene 5, as again in Scene 11 of the Berlin production, the compassionate material was contradicted by a style of acting more commonly found in farce. The sequence in which the Chaplain, having removed the plank from Kattrin, picks up Mother Courage and plonks her on a chest is reminiscent of episodes in early film comedies that culminate in the big policeman's intervention in a fight between two little men. Even more noteworthy is the confrontation, the staging of which Brecht describes:

> Still struggling with the chaplain, Courage sees her daughter rush into the house that is threatening to cave in, to save a baby. Tugged both ways, between Kattrin and the officers' shirts, she runs about until the shirts are torn into bandages and Kattrin comes out of the house with the infant. Now she runs after Kattrin to make her get rid of the baby. (Movements: Kattrin with the baby runs counter-clockwise around the wounded, then clockwise around the wagon.) *(p. 363)*

The shall-I-shan't-I dithering of Mother Courage is almost as staple a figure in farce as the ensuing chase routine. There is a splendid archive photograph of Kattrin, centre-stage and wrapped in the swirl of her skirt, about to weave round the wagon (clockwise) with Weigel downstage in hot pursuit. Just opening up to her view is the Chaplain, lumbering away from the wagon ripping a shirt. It is an effort to remember that the disputed property is an endangered baby and the obstacle around which the players manoeuvre is a mutilated peasant. The on-stage action is played *against* the material.

It is in Scene 5 that the smouldering relationship between mother and daughter bursts into flame. It will flare again in Scene 9. But Kattrin's condition of hostile dependence is a constant element in the play, from the moment in Scene 1 when Mother Courage disregards Kattrin's pantomime and loses Eilif, through the similar disregard in Scene 3 that contributes to Swiss Cheese's capture, to the climax of Kattrin's death and the anti-climax of Scene 12. It is not love but circumstance that keeps them together: but Brecht might reasonably have asked how often, in reality, love and circumstance are confused. In the Berlin production, Scene 5 ended with the two women alone on stage: 'At the end of the scene Kattrin lifted the baby into the air, while Courage rolled up the fur coat and threw it into the wagon: both women had their share of the spoils' (p. 365). Mother Courage is four shirts and a measure of schnapps down and one fur coat up, and Kattrin is in temporary possession of a child.

SCENE 6

In Scene 5 the Catholic General Tilly was triumphant. In Scene 6, a year later, he is dead, but Mother Courage's business prospers. It makes no difference to her whether her clients are Catholic or Protestant. As the rehearsal breakdown implies, the characteristic pace of this scene is slow, though quickened twice by Kattrin:

> Mother Courage, grown prosperous, is taking inventory; funeral oration for the fallen field marshal Tilly. Conversation about the duration of the war; the chaplain proves that the war is going to go on for a long time. Kattrin is sent to buy merchandise. Mother Courage declines a proposal of marriage and insists on firewood. Kattrin is permanently disfigured by some soldiers and rejects Yvette's shoes. Mother Courage curses the war. (*p. 366*)

The big event, Tilly's funeral, is taking place off-stage and Mother Courage, despite the promise of the opening caption, is not attending it. She has the trappings of her bourgeois status to sort out. The war has brought her to her native Bavaria, but that excites no comment from her. The play, like the war, takes small notice of geography.

Scene 3 opened with Mother Courage and Kattrin folding linen; Scene 6 opens comparably with the same pair taking an inventory of the stock. Around the action hangs the possibility that Tilly's death will provoke an outbreak of peace. If it does, Mother Courage will lose most of her market. She has to decide whether to buy in supplies, which are particularly cheap at the moment. It is in those terms that she and the Chaplain discuss the war. It is his cynical confidence in the people's ability to keep fighting that persuades her to purchase. She has changed, Brecht insists. 'Increasing prosperity has made her softer and more human' (p. 367). Perhaps, but the change is not easily perceptible. The issue of peace causes a rift between mother and daughter. 'I promised her she'd get a husband when peace comes' is Mother Courage's slightly mocking explanation of Kattrin's disappointment after she has heard the Chaplain's persuasive argument for the longevity of war. And there is more cruelty than softness in the way she packs Kattrin off to collect the supplies: 'Look sharp, don't let them take anything away from you, think of your dowry.' It is after this fashion that the widow teases the reluctant virgin.

Marriage is a theme in Scene 6. But if Kattrin's view of it is conventionally romantic, the Chaplain's is altogether more temperate. The sight of Mother Courage sucking at the Cook's pipe excites sexual rivalry in this randy man of God. It ought to be clear in the playing that his proposal of marriage has a commercial edge. He wants to share the profits instead of merely providing the labour. That, certainly, is how Mother Courage reads it:

> What'll you do if I'm ruined? See? You don't know. Chop that wood, then we'll be warm in the evening, which is a good thing in times like these.

And at that moment the scarred Kattrin stumbles in. She has saved the supplies but lost any prospect of marriage. It is now that we see once again the play's most colourful property, Yvette's red shoes. Mother Courage plucks them out of the wagon, planning to use them like toys to distract a sobbing child; but Kattrin understands all too clearly the significance of the sexual reference. Hurwicz had her crawl into the wagon like a mortally wounded animal, leaving Mother Courage to conclude, with brutal honesty, 'She can stop waiting for peace . . . and she's so crazy about children.' While cursing the war, Mother Courage sorts through the supplies that will help to sustain it. As C. V. Wedgwood observed, 'The provision of food in a starving country was the guiding consideration of warfare.'[11]

SCENE 7

'In this short scene', Brecht reports, 'Weigel showed Courage in the full possession of her vitality' (p. 370). The necklace of silver talers is the visible sign of her prosperity, and the song she sings declares her preference, if there's a war about, for getting involved in it. At the end of the previous scene she cursed the war, but now 'Mother Courage has corrected her opinion of the war and sings its praises as a good provider' (p. 369). Her recognition that the weak lose in peacetime as well as in war is another way of saying that, in the competitive conditions of capitalism, peace is nothing more or less than war undeclared. Brecht's 'scientific' theatre would be dedicated to the eradication of this anomalous state of affairs. He would have agreed with Eric Hobsbawm that human beings are 'not efficiently designed for a capitalist system of production'.[12]

SCENE 8

In so far as they are more or less continuous in time, Scenes 6–9 form a discrete unit within the play, part of whose narrative is the triangular tale of Mother Courage, the Cook and the Chaplain. We have reached the year 1632, when Gustavus Adolphus followed Tilly to an early grave. Eight years have passed since the play began, and Mother Courage cannot know that, having reached the height of her prosperity, she is about to begin her long slide towards destitution. Brecht's rehearsal analysis of Scene 8 is as follows:

Plate 3 Helene Weigel displays the striding vigour of her Mother Courage at the height of her prosperity.

Courage and the chaplain hear a rumour that peace has broken out. The cook reappears. The fight for the feedbag. An old friend who has made a good thing of the war; Pete the Pipe is unmasked. The downfall of Eilif, Mother Courage's brave son; he is executed for one of the misdeeds that had brought him rewards during the war. The peace comes to an end; Courage leaves the chaplain and goes on with the cook in the wake of the Swedish army.   (*p. 370*)

'The fight for the feedbag' is the competition between the Cook and the Chaplain for a place in Mother Courage's wagon-team. It is three years since the Cook disappeared, promising to be 'back for a little chat in a day or two' and leaving his pipe as a reminder. Mother Courage's preference for him is in doubt to no one, except sometimes the Chaplain, who himself fails woefully as a suitor. There is something unavoidably touching about the Chaplain's blundering attempts to impress Mother Courage. Without his robes of office, he is a figure of fun, and it is noticeable that it is not the coming of peace but the coming of the Cook that provokes his decision to don his clerical robes again. That will remind Mother Courage that he's a man to be reckoned with. In the event, though, his cockfight with the Cook is over before it really begins. Left alone while the Chaplain changes his clothes, the Cook and Mother Courage cross to a wooden bench in front of the wagon. 'Amid the ringing of bells they sit there almost like lovers, telling each other about the bankruptcy that peace has brought them' (p. 371). Hinz as the Chaplain (Geschonneck, too) reappeared in his clerical garb and moved to the centre of the stage – like an actor displaying his favourite outfit at a costume parade – but faltered to a halt as he sensed the atmosphere. In Brecht's colourful phrase, he stood 'like a last incisor in a toothless mouth' (p. 371). More than anyone else in the play he has represented the role of the bourgeois intelligentsia in the Thirty Years War. As such, his welcoming of the peace is no more impressive than his apologia for the war. He is a time-server whose attempt at self-assertion cuts no ice with Mother Courage. When she takes exception to his dangerously accurate description of her as a 'battlefield hyena', he tries to hold his ground, but the stage-grouping is against him. He is the outsider, isolated and more than a little forlorn. Left alone with the phlegmatic Cook, the Chaplain threatens murder. The Cook unwraps his bandaged feet imperturbably, demonstrating a confidence that he has found his resting-place, and the Chaplain crumbles:

> Hinz as the chaplain obtained a powerful and natural effect when, suddenly throwing all his arrogance to the winds, he begged the cook not to squeeze him out of his place with Courage, because, having become a better man, he could no longer practise the clergyman's profession. His fear of losing his job lent him a new dignity. (*p. 372*)

The dignity to which Brecht refers is nothing to do with the actor's demeanour. It is the despairing recognition of the character that he now belongs to a despised and rejected underclass. The actor must determine whether this recognition endures.

The confrontation of the Cook and the Chaplain is interrupted by the entry of Yvette Pottier, hideously transformed; the prelude to a recognition (*anagnorisis*) that, in the Aristotelean theatre, would have changed the direction of the plot. *Theaterarbeit* contains adjacent photographs of Regine Lutz, who played Yvette in the 1951 revival.[13] In the first (Scene 3) she is provocatively *décolletée*, fresh-faced and vigorous. In the second, as the widowed Countess Stahremberg, she is plastered with make-up, obviously bald under a black wig, bloated, twisted, and walking with the aid of a stick. Brecht had several shots at giving Yvette a precise age. In the 'authoritative' text she is only twenty-four in Scene 8, though an alternative version would have her thirty-nine. Either way, she is not so much a character in fictional history as a demonstration of the high price little people must pay for success in the competitive market. Her advent stimulates in the 'dignified' Chaplain an unworthy hope that his rival will lose favour with Mother Courage, but Yvette's attack on her seducer turns out to be counter-productive. If Mother Courage is going to take another sexual partner she would prefer a potent one. As she assures the Cook at the end of the scene, 'It hasn't lowered you in my estimation. Far from it. Where there's smoke there's fire. Coming?' By then the Chaplain has taken his undistinguished final exit. (This fading away of a major character is a feature of Brecht's distinctly un-Aristotelean dramaturgy.) Mother Courage will not miss him, but his departure is another among a succession of losses that will leave her, at the play's end, bare.

The loss of Eilif would touch her more deeply if she were ever to hear of it. 'He's my favourite', she explains – with characteristic carelessness in the hearing of Kattrin. It chances that Mother Courage is off-stage for the duration of Eilif's brief reappearance, his stay of execution. It is, perhaps, a wild hope that she will pluck salvation out of nowhere that has brought him to his mother at this final crisis. More than anyone else, more even than the Cook, Eilif upholds the myth of Mother Courage's infinite resourcefulness. In reality she achieves very little beyond the sale of a capon in Scene 2 and two stricken years on the road with the Cook – a romantic idyll marred by the gooseberry presence of the disfigured Kattrin. The Cook's failure to report Eilif's death to Mother Courage is uncannily dramatic. It is, properly played, a supreme example of the acting technique which Brecht classified as the 'not . . . but . . . '. The actor, whilst showing us what the character actually did, also draws our attention to what the character did not do. In this case the Cook did *not* tell Mother Courage of Eilif's death *but* helped her pack the wagon. In packing the wagon he shows us that he might have told her of Eilif's death. Nothing is inevitable. People can change. People can change the world.

SCENE 9

Scenes 5 and 11 are the only ones without a song. Since Scenes 3 and 12 have two, there are twelve songs altogether; enough, almost, to have *Mother Courage* classified as a musical. But the songs are not intrinsic to the style of the play: they obtrude, call attention to themselves, disrupt the action. The song in Scene 9 is a warning against the deadly virtues – of wisdom, daring, honesty, unselfishness, and the fear of God. These are qualities that in various ways shore up the status quo. It is a set-piece, inserted into a scene of gritty dialogue which Brecht breaks down as follows:

> The cook has inherited a tavern in Utrecht. Kattrin hears the cook refuse to take her along to Utrecht. The 'Song of the Temptations of the Great'. Kattrin decides to spare her mother the need to make a decision, packs her bundle and leaves a message. Mother Courage stops Kattrin from running away and goes on alone with her. The cook goes to Utrecht. (*p. 374*)

Two years have passed, and the wagoners are reduced to begging for food. It is an exceptionally severe winter, and the Cook and Mother Courage are wearing shabby sheepskins. This, in the Berlin production, was the first occasion on which Mother Courage herself was harnessed to the wagon. Bildt, as the Cook, unharnessed himself 'morosely' and proposed to Mother Courage that they should go to Utrecht, away from the war-zone and, therefore, necessarily out of the play. What the Cook ignores, and what we cannot fail to notice, is that this is another *three*-character scene. Indeed, Kattrin's attitude of overhearing (which Brecht might call her characteristic *gest* of listening) dominates the scene for the audience. In an important note, Brecht comments:

> In this scene the cook must not under any circumstances be represented as brutal. The tavern he has inherited is too small to keep three people, and the customers cannot be expected to put up with the sight of the disfigured Kattrin. Courage does not find his arguments unreasonable. (*p. 375*)

Nevertheless, she rejects them. During the begging song Weigel made it plain that she was thinking things over. Her sexual partnership with the Cook is at risk, and she is seriously contemplating selling the wagon and presumably 'losing' Kattrin. But by the end of the song she has decided to decline the Cook's offer, and she goes into the presbytery just for the soup. It is now that Kattrin, through the lewdly symbolic placing of the Cook's trousers on top of Mother Courage's skirt, supplies her own verdict on the scene. Hers is a combination of altruism (she 'decides to spare her mother the need to make a decision') and disgust. Hurwicz accompanied the action with a barely stifled 'uncanny, malignant giggle' (p. 376). Yet again the motherhood of Mother Courage is under scrutiny in this scene. How far do we believe her own disavowal: 'don't go thinking I've given him the gate on your account. It's the wagon, I'm used to it, it's not you, it's the wagon.' On the first of these sentences Weigel pushed a spoonful of soup into Hurwicz's mouth. Brecht's note on the staging of the scene's final moments indicates the careful pacing of the Berlin production:

> Scenes of this kind must be fully acted out: Courage and Kattrin harness themselves to the wagon, push it back a few feet so as to be able to circle the presbytery, and then move off to the right. The cook comes out, still chewing on a piece of bread, sees his belongings, picks them up and goes off to the rear with long steps. We see him disappear. Thus the parting of the ways is made visible. (*p. 376*)

Another minor exit for a major character: Ernst Busch, who played the Cook after 1951, indicated the sexual significance of the parting by letting his pipe first droop and then fall from his mouth. Mother Courage, still hoping for a sighting of Eilif, does not know that Kattrin is all that remains of her world – Kattrin and the depleted wagon. She dare not forsake the war for a home.

SCENE 10

This short scene consists, visually, of the pulling on of the wagon by Mother Courage and Kattrin, their silent pause, and then their pulling off of the wagon. It represents a year in harness, a year during which the two women have been unable to catch up with the armies. The wagon is as poverty-stricken as they are. It has been a year in which, though Mother Courage might speak, there has been no one to answer. This too, for a woman whose mercantile rhythms have been punctuated by conversation, is a deprivation. The off-stage song celebrates domestic stability, but the two women observed by the audience are homeless. Brecht reports a 'fine variation' when he worked on the play in Munich in 1950: 'the song was sung with unfeeling, provocative self-assurance. The arrogant pride of possession expressed in the singing turned the listeners on the road into damned souls' (p. 376). He did not wish the actors to betray their feelings as they listened to the song – 'the audience can imagine' (p. 377). One (or both?) of them is surely thinking of an inn in Utrecht.

SCENE 11

This is one of the greatest single scenes ever written, and it is, perhaps, unsurprising that Brecht was always a little embarrassed by it. He must, after all, have been aware that he had beaten the pathos-seekers at their own game. Certainly there is a shifty quality in much of his *post hoc* explication:

> If the scene is to be saved from a wild excitement amid which every-thing worth noticing is lost, close attention must be given to aliena-tion.
>
> For example: if the conversation of the peasants is swallowed up by a general hubbub, the audience will be in danger of being 'carried away'; then they will fail to notice how the peasants justify their failure to act, how they fortify each other in the belief that there is nothing they can do, so that the only remaining possibility of 'action' becomes prayer. (*pp. 379–80*)

Brecht might have believed that people would be less likely to be carried away by the pathos of Kattrin's death if they were to adopt a critical attitude towards the peasants, but I doubt it. What he was particularly anxious to make clear is that the scene, despite the domination of the Kattrin narrative, is not without its contradictions. The rehearsal breakdown, however, does little to disturb Kattrin's dramatic centrality:

> A surprise attack is planned on the city of Halle; soldiers force a young peasant to show them the way. The peasant and his wife tell Kattrin to join them in praying for the city. Kattrin climbs up on the barn roof and beats the drum to awaken the city. Neither the offer to spare her mother in the city nor the threat to smash the wagon can make her stop drumming. Kattrin's death. (*p. 377*)

Brecht may not fully have recognised the extent to which the fortunes of Kattrin had gripped his imagination, but the actress Hurwicz obviously did. After her mutilation in Scene 6, Hurwicz's Kattrin became paranoiacally shy of being seen by men. She hides in the wagon whenever she can, and when forced out of hiding, as she is by the Cook in Scene 8 and by the soldiers in this scene, she employs a futile gesture of concealment. This gesture was Hurwicz's invention, and Brecht approved of it, but he remained nervous of the psychological speculations her mute heroism might inspire in the audience, and endeavoured to impede them:

> The whole point is missed if her love of children is depreciated as mindless animal instinct. Her saving of the city of Halle is an intelligent act. How else would it be possible to bring out what must be brought out, namely, that here the most helpless creature of all is ready to help? (*p. 365*)

The question is not entirely honest. Brecht must have known that the point he is here stressing makes itself in performance, regardless of the issue of Kattrin's intelligence. If Kattrin appears in any way intelligent, it is only because of the stupidity of the Catholic soldiers whom she outwits.

Kattrin's death is, by any reckoning, an emotional climax, and Hurwicz was encouraged to play it to the full. There is an archival photograph of the melodramatically splayed death-gesture, and Brecht's commentary records that 'Kattrin falls forward, the drumsticks in her drooping hands strike one full beat followed by a feeble beat' (p. 378). Surprisingly, what he neglects to stress is the near-knockabout comedy that contradicts the solemnity of the scene. The soldiers' attempts to dislodge Kattrin from the roof are risible enough, but their resolution to prevent the drum's sound from alerting the citizens of Halle by drowning it with *more* noise launches us into the realms of farce. This wonderful scene is a symphony of sound effects, to which the cannon of the awakened city provides the final chords.

SCENE 12

It is in the writing of the final scene that Brecht risks converting a lucid, historicised play into a tragedy. The actor of Mother Courage must preserve a sense of proportion. If she loses objectivity, gets involved *in* rather than maintaining an attitude *to* the loneliness of Mother Courage, the audience will leave the theatre with a final impression of a woman who, having endured the worst the world can do to her, has come through. They will have failed to notice that it need not have ended like this. The responsibility for delivering the play rests with the actors, and Brecht gives them an escape-route from his politics. Almost recklessly, even in his rehearsal breakdown, he carries the play to the edge of tears:

> The peasants have to convince Courage that Kattrin is dead. The lullaby for Kattrin. Mother Courage pays for Kattrin's burial and receives the condolences of the peasants. Alone, Mother Courage harnesses herself to the empty wagon; still hoping to get back into business, she follows the ragged army. (*p. 381*)

The peasants do not like Mother Courage. She belongs, for them, to the exploiting classes – and she has put their meagre livelihood at risk. Unlike those who attend King Lear, they are untouched by the parent's evident belief that the dead child is alive. Weigel played the scene with a clear sense of the risks involved. She sang the lullaby 'without any sentimentality':

> By slight emphasis on the 'you', Weigel portrayed Courage's treacherous hope of bringing her child, and perhaps hers alone, through the war. To this child who had lacked even the most ordinary things, she promised the most extraordinary. (*p. 383*)

Brecht also credits Weigel with the invention of one particularly indicative piece of stage-business:

> Even in paying for the burial, Weigel gave one last hint of Courage's character. She fished a few coins out of her leather bag, put one back and gave the peasants the rest. This did not in the least detract from the overpowering effect of desolation. (*p. 383*)

Such are the rewards of maintaining an attitude towards the character you are playing.

In the Berlin production the house and barn – set-pieces for Scene 11 – were struck, leaving the wagon alone on stage. In response to another suggestion from Weigel, this production had begun with a prologue, showing the full family on their way to the war-zone; Eilif and Swiss Cheese drawing the wagon with Mother Courage and Kattrin in it. That is to say that the performance had begun with the wagon alone on an empty stage and would now end in the same way – the same, but different. The visual echo was a forceful indication of changed circumstances. When the peasants have left the stage, Mother Courage 'goes to the wagon, unrolls the cord which Kattrin had until then been pulling, takes a stick, examines it, pulls the loop of the second cord through, wedges a stick under her arm and moves off'. It is a slow procedure, further protracted in performance:

> Of course the audience would understand if it were simply pulled
> away. When it goes on rolling there is a moment of irritation . . .
> But when it goes on still longer, a deeper understanding sets in.
> (*pp. 383–4*)

It should not escape our notice that she can get the wagon moving
without assistance only because it is virtually empty.

CHAPTER THREE

THE BERLIN PRODUCTION: 1949

To a unique extent among plays of the modern era, the text of *Mother Courage* has been identified with a single production – Brecht's own with the Berliner Ensemble and with Helene Weigel as Mother Courage. That is partly because of the claims of the Model Book, a richly provocative and, in the pre-electronic age, sophisticated documentation of rehearsal processes and performance. But it is also because the production, variously adjusted, had a long life. Held in repertoire for a decade, it was staged over 400 times, not only in Berlin but across Europe. Indeed, it was the award of first prize to *Mother Courage* at the first Paris Festival International d'Art Dramatique in July 1954 that established the Berliner Ensemble as one of Europe's leading theatrical companies; and the preservation of the production in the 1961 filming of it has made it available for reference. Subsequent productions have this one looking over their shoulders. At worst, the outcome has been to threaten the play with the status of a museum-piece. Already in 1950 Mother Courage's wagon was a familiar icon in East Berlin. It had pride of place that year on the Berliner Ensemble's float in the Mayday procession, with Brecht's nineteen-year-old daughter Barbara sitting on it, waving a red flag. Later it became a museum exhibit. When a single production can so readily be presented as if it were definitive, it is not always easy to remember that it belonged, and belongs, to a particular place at a particular time.

The place was the Deutsches Theater, an unpretentious building set back from a side-street which connects the Charité Hospital to the eighteenth-century Friedrichstrasse. Originally designed as the city's grand imperial highway, the Friedrichstrasse had already surrendered its supremacy by 1905, when Max Reinhardt took over as director of the Deutsches Theater. The side-street now bears Reinhardt's name. During the rehearsals in late 1948, Brecht could pick his way there from the semi-derelict Hotel Adlon where he and Weigel were for several months guests of the *Kulturbund*, the official cultural union of the Communist Party. The Adlon had been one of the splendours of old Berlin. The Kaiser had favoured it, as had the cultured socialite Count Harry Kessler. Gerhart Hauptmann always stayed there on his visits to Berlin, when it was the most expensive hotel in the city. Later, Unity Mitford had made it the Berlin headquarters for her extravagant plot to marry Hitler and unite Britain with Germany. On the night of the Reichstag fire in 1933, it was housing an I. G. Farben conference. The delegates could see from their meeting-room the flames that reached above the Brandenburg Gate. Soon Hitler would be arranging for guests of state to be accommodated in the Hotel Adlon. And now Brecht! The irony did not escape him, nor did the awareness of his privileged status as an artist in the Soviet sector of the city. On 6 December 1948 he wrote to Kurt Weill in America, with the pardonable exaggeration of a homecomer addressing one who had chosen to remain in exile:

> Living conditions here are not at all bad for artists, the picture the
> newspapers have painted of Berlin is ridiculous. I'm living at the
> Adlon, eating as usual, keeping reasonably warm, etc. Of course
> we theatre people have a good many privileges.[1]

The reality for most of the population was not so rosy. Brecht's route to the Deutsches Theater took him past bomb craters and gutted houses and across the temporary bridge over the River Spree. Signs of hunger and poverty were everywhere. He observed them every day during his deliberate fifteen-minute walk from the Hotel Adlon to the rehearsal room. Three days after the letter to Weill, he noted in his journal:

> everywhere in this great city, where everything is always in flux, no
> matter how little and how provisional that 'everything' happens at the

moment to be, the new german *misere* is apparent, which is that nothing has been eliminated even when almost everything has been destroyed . . . and the workers never reflect that hitler's war of destruction against the soviet union was waged without their being consulted, though not without their participation; and the jobs created by rearmament met with the acclaim of a great number of them.[2]

It was the definitive intention of the play he was rehearsing when he made that observation to impel reflection on social change and the possibility of choice; but, for the rubble-pickers he passed on his way to rehearsal, bread was a higher priority.

The Hotel Adlon was the first building on the right when you entered the Soviet sector of Berlin. A new kind of war was already being waged to the west of the adjacent Brandenburg Gate. It was initiated by aggressive capitalism, and its outward manifestation was prosperity. What has come to be internationally known as the 'cold' war was noticeably hot in Berlin. The Berlin Airlift, America's effective response to the Soviet blockade of land access to the city, had been in progress for several months when Brecht and Weigel took up residence in the Hotel Adlon. On 27 October 1948 Brecht noted that 'above the silent streets of ruins the freight planes of the airlift drone in the night'.[3] The refurbishment of West Berlin was an important item on the post-war American agenda. An East Berliner could, by Christmas 1948, board a bus in the Friedrichstrasse, where ruined buildings proclaimed a defeated country, and travel to the Kurfürstendamm, which was already looking like a shopping parade for the victors. Not until 1953 would the sector boundaries be closed to buses and trams, although telephone links between East and West Berlin had been severed the previous year. The contrast was excellent propaganda for capitalism. In the unceasing war between the have-nots and the haves, the active belligerents – except in the rare event of a revolution or the commoner outbreak of a riot – are always the haves. West Berliners among the first audiences of *Mother Courage* might well have felt smug as they approached the Deutsches Theater along bomb-scarred streets and past crumbling buildings. In April

1949, with *Mother Courage* in its third month, the North Atlantic Treaty Organisation was established. In May the Soviet Union abandoned its thwarted attempt to blockade Berlin. Two weeks later West Germany pronounced itself a Federal Republic, with Berlin as its hook in the Soviet-controlled bloc. For most Germans, still hoping for prompt reunification, it was a realised nightmare. Not until October were Stalin and Walter Ulbricht ready with their riposte of a 'Democratic Republic'. By then, after several exploratory months in Zürich, Brecht had committed himself, at least for a while, to Berlin.

That commitment was by no means certain on 11 January 1949, when *Mother Courage* had its official opening night. This was not yet a performance by the Berliner Ensemble, although Weigel was already working to recruit a permanent company. On the contrary, Brecht had assembled a scratch cast, only a few known to him in advance. Like most directors he preferred to work with actors whose methods he knew and approved. Unlike most directors he had an ideological and emotional preference for collective endeavour. Because his own personality was so dominant, a Brecht collective could always appear, particularly to hostile observers, like a clique around a guru. Insiders tell a different story, and the effect of the passage of time on those of Brecht's associates who have recorded their experience has made it difficult to distinguish between the eventual practice of the Berliner Ensemble and the processes that went towards the 1949 performance of *Mother Courage*. The production was built around a nucleus of Weigel, Paul Bildt as the Cook, Werner Hinz as the Chaplain and Angelika Hurwicz as Kattrin. Brecht had worked with Bildt before and considered him 'undoubtedly the greatest actor in Germany'.[4] Hinz was well known from his screen performances. The extraordinary Hurwicz was a largely unknown quantity, but she would become a key figure in the Ensemble. Two old associates, Gerhard Bienert and Gerda Müller, agreed to appear in the small roles of the Sergeant (Scene 1) and the Peasant Woman (Scenes 11 and 12), signalling a generosity of attitude that ought to characterise any ensemble. Most reassuring of all, perhaps, was the presence of Erich Engel as co-director. Engel had directed several of Brecht's earlier plays, including (famously) the first production of *The Threepenny Opera*, and he knew and understood Brecht's collective impulse. But it was impossible to cast the play entirely from the pool of actors already known to Brecht or Weigel. There was only a handful available in East Berlin, and all of them middle-aged by now. A generation of young actors had grown up in Germany during the fifteen years of Brecht's exile, and it was particularly to find the younger members of the cast of thirty-two that auditions were held in early November 1948. Among other things, Brecht was looking for actors capable of delivering to an audience the songs, with Dessau's unfamiliar settings. Andreas Meyer-Hanno records an indicative response:

> I'll never forget his remarks after auditioning one of many candidates for the role of Yvette . . . This particular singer, a product of 'classical' training, tried to show off her vocal technique. But when she left the room, Brecht said to my mother, 'Terrible! She has gone and learned how to sing, and now she can't sing any more.'[5]

Because he was trying to bring back to the post-war Berlin stage a production-style that had been outlawed under the Nazis, Brecht's task was not an easy one.

He was alerted to the scale of the problem on his second day in the city, when he attended the première of Gyula Hay's *Haben* at the Deutsches Theater. Against the tide of critical acclaim, Brecht found it an 'appalling performance, hysterical and stilted, totally unrealistic'.[6] The inflated style which had been demanded of the younger actors during their novitiate in Nazi Germany was assimilated, with surprising ease, into the approved aesthetic of the Communist Party – the 'socialist realism' initially enforced by Zhdanov at the Soviet Writers' Congress in 1934. The realism which Brecht advocated flouted the Zhdanovite scriptures, exciting the hostility, among many other Marxist critics, of Georg Lukács, the cultured

Hungarian high priest of socialist realism. *Mother Courage*, with its frequent reminders to the audience that it *is* an audience, and an audience *in a theatre*, and that *therefore* it is incumbent on it to test theatrical fiction against contemporary reality, has its part to play in the dispute between Lukács and Brecht.[7] For devotees of the Party line, the play was formalist, not socialist realist. 'You call this art?', Otto Grotewohl, first President of the German Democratic Republic, is said to have asked when he eventually saw *Mother Courage*.[8] Brecht understood Grotewohl's position much better than Grotewohl understood his:

> what you are running into [he told himself] is the desire that artistic expression should merely be heightened expression, and should not turn into a different quality, namely that of art. they want people to write – or paint, or make music – from the heart.[9]

Since he preferred to write from the head, it was fortunate for Brecht that he was a potent weapon in the propaganda war, one that the East German state would not want to fall into enemy hands. From 1949 until his death in 1956, he sailed as close to the wind as could reasonably have been expected of him. He had no taste for martyrdom and no inclination to strike heroic postures, but he maintained a stubborn confidence in his own artistic authority, and he took the theatre very seriously indeed. His realism, unlike socialist realism, had designs on the audience rather than on the Soviet praesidium, but he was already anticipating official criticism during the rehearsals of *Mother Courage*:

> as long as by realism one understands a style and not an attitude, one is nothing other than a formalist. a realistic artist is one whose works of art adopt an attitude that brings results. (one part of an artist's reality is his public.)[10]

Brecht knew full well that the authorities would pay no heed to his counter-charge that socialist realism leads to formalism.

The production of *Mother Courage* offered Brecht a twofold opportunity: firstly, to test his developing theatrical aesthetic with a company (not yet a collective) of his own choosing, and secondly, to signal to the communist authorities that, if he were to be offered a significant subsidy, he might lend his name to a theatre company in East Berlin. There was a lot at stake between November 1948 and the scheduled opening in January of the following year. Under the circumstances, Brecht displayed surprisingly little political caution. He might, for example, have camouflaged his innovations with conventionally tuneful music or acceptably artistic scenery. He did neither.

Paul Dessau had written much of the *Courage* music in America in 1946. According to Brecht, it is not meant to be easy: 'like the stage set, it left something to be supplied by the audience' (p. 335). Dessau's musical mode is not readily accessible. Brecht knew and approved that, and he relished Dessau's willingness to be led. We can assume, then, that Brecht considered the nervy tone-language of the score an appropriately contradictory element in the production. The Party faithful thought its dissonance 'formalist' – the word always trotted out to describe artistic failure – and most of the actors had trouble with the timing of the songs. Weigel had daily meetings with the theatre's musical adviser, who coached her through the complex rhythms. Hans Werner Henze, who came to know Dessau and his music well, found the 'charismatic agitation' of the man mirrored in the music.[11] Much of his *Courage* music might fairly be described as 'agitated', and Brecht enjoyed those occasions, for example in 'The Song of the Great Capitulation', when the confidence of the sung words was contradicted and undermined (alienated) by the jarring of the music. Even so, as the play's performance history has shown, Dessau's music is more easily detachable from *Mother Courage* than Weill's is from any and Eisler's is from most of the Brecht plays they worked on. Whatever Brecht and Dessau felt, a symbiotic relationship has not been historically established. In the longer term, the original music has proved less significant than the original decision over the deployment of the musicians. In the Deutsches Theater they were positioned in a box adjacent to the stage: 'thus their performances became little concerts, independent contributions made at suitable points in the play' (p. 336). In London's Royal National Theatre production in 1995, the music was composed by Jonathan Dove, not Dessau, but the musicians occupied a box adjacent to the stage. The songs in *Mother Courage* are occasions for strategic interruption of the narrative. Such interruptions are, at their simplest, reminders to the audience that it is not witnessing the imitation of an action, but the representation of a series of discontinuous actions. It is implicit, in a seamless narrative, that its consecutive episodes must be causally linked. The next thing is consequential on the thing before. By interrupting the action, Brecht opens causality to question. By disturbing the easy relationship between words and music, Dessau was attempting to carry the disruption into another realm of aesthetics.

Brecht expressed himself more satisfied with the music than with the set for *Mother Courage*. His attempts to bring his favourite designer and close friend, Caspar Neher, to East Berlin failed, and Heinrich Kilger was at best a tolerated substitute. The problem is essentially one of role-definition. The German word for a scene, *Bild*, is also the common word for a picture. That is to say that 'picture' is its primary meaning. It is also the word for a frame in a film, for the outward impression of a thing seen (which may or may not contradict its totality) and, by association, for a metaphor or even for an idea, as in the English idiom 'I get the picture.' In his work with Neher, Brecht had glimpsed the possibility of fusing this complex of meanings in the functional art of the stage-designer. The stage-picture conveys the idea of the scene or episode; the theatrical metaphor impinges on life outside the theatre; a frozen frame conveys socially significant attitudes. The working method of Brecht and Neher involved dialogue that continued through rehearsals. Neher's artistic dexterity enabled him to express his ideas about a play through sketches of possible stage configurations. These *Arrangementskizzen* were not records of a play-text's present meaning but contributions to a possible future meaning, to be tested in rehearsal. In 1950, when Neher did work with Brecht on the Berliner Ensemble's production of *The Tutor*, Egon Monk noticed that Neher 'would say nothing about a space till he knew what was supposed to take place in it':

> Neher's sketches anticipated a production by a particular director with particular actors and a particular Ensemble. They were not interchangeable, decorations for some production or other with conceivable alternatives. He was not sketching 'stage pictures' but the play.[12]

It was unfortunate for Brecht that Neher was unable to be in Berlin to assist in the rehearsals of *Mother Courage* at the end of 1948, all the more so because Neher had already worked on the play. The surviving sketches of his ideas for the 1946 revival at the Zürich Schauspielhaus have a gaiety that was largely absent from the Deutsches Theater production. The same is true of the drawings he made towards the subsequently abandoned film-project, for which Brecht had such high hopes in his early Berlin days. The dynamic interaction between Brecht and Neher proved to be unrepeatable with other designers, although Brecht appreciated Karl Von Appen's Neher-inspired approach to the 1954 production of *The Caucasian Chalk Circle*. As Christopher Baugh has lucidly outlined in an important essay, 'contemporary theatre has learnt from and extended Brecht's fundamental concept of scenography as active performance'.[13]

It was partly in order to maintain the pressure on Neher to come to Berlin that Brecht complained to him, in a letter dated 28 January 1949, that 'the *Courage* set was no good. We waited for you till the last moment and then had to improvise.' Kilger, in fact, did an honest job according to his brief. That brief was essentially to realise Teo Otto's designs for the 1941 Zürich première, on the understanding that they could not be improved in the time available. Otto had immediately perceived that the positioning of the wagon in successive scenes would determine the scope of the actors' movement; an obvious enough point in retrospect, but one whose application required an architect's feeling for space and logistics.

Otto's scenic innovation was to employ his set-pieces sparsely. He used 'real' materials – tenting, wooden posts, ropes – and even the three-dimensional buildings were, as Brecht observed, artistically abbreviated: 'only so much being shown as was necessary for the action' (p. 336). This, in East Berlin in 1949, was a flouting of socialist realism, a formalist statement of the primacy of art. For Brecht, the true realism was in the acting.

Brecht's delight in the artistry of actors is one of the most attractive features of his theatre practice. He gave credit to their inventiveness and liked to record outstanding examples of it. These examples without exception reveal the actors' translation into physical terms of their thinking about the social implications of a role. *Gestus* is the definitive term here. By his use of it, Brecht aimed to describe the actors' conscious application to their on-stage behaviour of their attitude to reality. Thus, because they are, after all, acting, the basic *Gestus* is the *Gestus* of showing. They do not attempt to mask reality in illusion. On the contrary, the aim is to go beyond Stanislavskian naturalism (the actor's 'truth' contained within the theatre-building) to realism (the actor's recognition of the relationship between the dramatic event and life outside the theatre). Ekkehard Schall, who played Eilif for the Ensemble in the 1950s and who became a major force in the company after Brecht's death, expresses a Brechtian actor's routine response:

> Tackling a new project presupposes that I'm really interested in the play or the role I'm going to act. Initially, this interest is not in the acting side, but in a problem inherent in the play – I mean a philosophical problem which must concern me personally and at the same time exist in the world outside my head, and which I try to solve in a social context through getting into the character I'm to play.[14]

But this was not a routine that came ready-made to the group of actors brought together to rehearse *Mother Courage* during the last months of the year 1948. Nor did Brecht have available the length of rehearsal-time that would be the expectation of the Ensemble, once established. There is a significant entry, dated 21 December 1948, in Brecht's journal:

> we really need four months of rehearsals. in these circumstances it isn't possible to make it epic. you cannot burden the actors with the process of lightening everything in so short a time.

The quest for 'lightness' is characteristic. It featured in Brecht's last message to the Berliner Ensemble, posted on the bulletin-board nine days before his death. The company was about to embark for England, where the long-lived production of *Mother Courage* was to be presented:

> . . . there is in England a long-standing fear that German art (literture, painting, music) must be terribly heavy, slow, laborious and pedestrian.
> So our playing needs to be quick, light, strong. This is not a question of hurry, but of speed, not simply of quick playing, but of quick thinking. We must keep the tempo of a run-through and infect it with quiet strength, with our own fun.[15]

The actor's enjoyment is part of the *Gestus* of showing. It was, in Brecht's view, because of a lack of rehearsal-time that there was too little of it in the 1949 première: 'Much was shown, but the element of showing was absent' (p. 386).

During its long stage-life, the production of *Mother Courage* evolved and 'lightened'. Recasting contributed something to the improvement, no so much because the new actors were better but because the process of rehearsing them into their parts enhanced the *Gestus* of showing:

> Here the actors 'demonstrated', that is, they showed the new members of the cast certain positions and tones, and the whole took on the wonderfully relaxed, effortless, and unobtrusive quality that stimu-lates the spectator to think and feel for himself.   (*p. 386*)

Although it was certainly the task of rehearsals to fix stage-group-ings, it was not the intention to fix every detail of the individual actor's performance. Those, like Weigel, who knew their purposes, Brecht trusted, and might celebrate their improvisations. The end of Scene 10 is a case in point:

> In one of the later performances Weigel, when starting off again, tossed her head and shook it like a tired draft horse getting back to work. It is doubtful whether this gesture can be imitated. (*p. 377*)

When lines or gestures were added in rehearsal but not included in the published text, it was because they were created by or for particular actors whose uniqueness Brecht respected. Nor should it be supposed that Brechtian acting was, or is, distinct at every moment from Stanislavskian acting. It is, ultimately, idle to try to determine whether the person who tossed and shook her head like a tired draft horse was Mother Courage or Helene Weigel; and Ekkehard Schall was not slipping his tongue when he spoke of 'getting into the character I'm to play'. The consistent distinction is that the epic actor is not bound down (or up) in the character. In one of the latest of his many observations on epic acting, dating from Christmas Day 1952, Brecht wrote:

> if you look soberly at what i have called epic acting, it is a type of acting that brings out the contradiction, which is there in the nature of things, between the actor and the character he is acting. the actor's (social) criticism of the figure, to whom he must naturally give full expression, comes into play. the opinions, passions, experiences, interests of the character are not of course those of the actor, and the latter have to come out in the acting. (that always happens, in the natural course of events, but there was to my knowledge little consciousness of it.)
>
> in this, as in various other matters, the entry of dialectics into the theatre triggered a perceptible shock among those who accepted dialectics in other areas.[16]

Brecht unreservedly admired Weigel's intelligence, and found in her the clearest evidence of the double exposure of actor and character. 'Weigel's way of playing Mother Courage was hard and angry,' he wrote, 'that is, her Mother Courage was not angry; she herself, the actress, was angry' (p. 388). The critical tension, a sort of temporarily contained hostility, between actor and character gave a disturbing edge to Weigel's performance. Courage's failure to learn was something she took personally.

Weigel acted sparely, with utter unfussiness. All that was unnecessary was eliminated. Käthe Rülicke-Weiler, then a new young member of the company, considered her on stage 'more ordinary than anybody else in the auditorium',[17] and if her lack of guile was artful, it was certainly not an art intended to deceive the audience. Her lack of interest in theories of acting was genuine. The theatre was her business, and her attitude to it was generally as matter-of-fact as Mother Courage's to war. Asked about the working methods of the Berliner Ensemble, she answered, 'We tell the story.'[18] Telling the story in the theatre is not, of course, a straightforward matter, but Weigel was here repeating the emphasis of Brecht's own practice. Everything in his production of *Mother Courage* was intended to contribute to the telling of the story. Movement and grouping on the stage were conceived in terms of narrative: Brecht referred to them under the heading of the 'story-telling arrangement'. His idea was that the 'fable' should be comprehensible to an audience that could see but not hear the play. Weigel shared Brecht's dramaturgical ambitions as well as his political ideology, and they both had designs on the audience. The story had to be told in such a way as to aid those designs, and that necessitated the disturbance of an audience's natural tendency to accept any story as logical and inevitable within its own terms. The whole purpose of the various *Verfremdungseffekte* – textual, musical, scenic – was to force the audience out of the slipstream of the narrative. As writer and director, Brecht laboured both to tell and to contradict a story, but the work could be completed only by the actors. Asked for an explanation of what the Ensemble actors understood by the word *Verfremdungseffekt*, Ekkehard Schall referred to the moment in Scene 6 of *Mother Courage* when 'Weigel while cursing the war checked the goods.'[19] He might have chosen many others. Weigel relished and embodied contradiction.

It was important to Brecht that thinking should not end when acting began. To lose the self in the part is to surrender responsibility for the play. Put simply, while Mother Courage acted (or failed to act), Weigel went on thinking. A largely thoughtless character was being enacted by a highly thoughtful person, and the contradiction between the two was the vital substance of the performance. It was intended to guide the audience towards a recognition that 'things as they are' are not 'things as they must be'. The human capacity to change the world exhibits itself, in Brecht's theatre, through actors who believe in it. The kind of thinking that Weigel applied to her playing of Mother Courage is, at root, interventionist.[20] The actor displays an attitude to social processes. It is an attitude which, if shared by the audience, might enforce a modification in or abandonment of those social processes. It is by reference to the idea of the actor – one who causes actions to occur – that Alain Touraine proposes his alternative approach to sociology:

> . . . a large part of sociology is still beholden to the nineteenth-century idea that society is an organic or a mechanical system, with its own laws, and that the function of sociological analysis is to dispel the illusion of the actor. Such an approach excludes the existence of social movements a priori. It is increasingly important to defend another sociology, one that gives a central role to the idea of social movement and creates a new professional practice that attempts to apprehend actors in the awareness of their action, a sociology for which human beings make history knowing that they do so.[21]

Touraine's sociological project was, in important ways, anticipated in the practice of the Berliner Ensemble. Rehearsals were conducted in such a way as to prepare actors, at any moment in performance, to be apprehended in the awareness of their action. They were to make history, knowing that they did so.

The means towards this political end were concrete and specific. Brecht's was never the consecrated theatre of Stanislavsky,

Grotowski or Peter Brook. In his journal entry for 10 December 1948, he noted:

> i put in 10 minutes epic rehearsal for the first time in the eleventh scene. gerda müller and dunskus as peasants are deciding that they cannot do anything against the catholics. i ask them to add 'said the man', 'said the woman' after each speech. suddenly the scene became clear and müller found a realistic attitude.[22]

Two days later there was a development to record:

> begin cautiously introducing the epic mode in rehearsals. the scenes begin to fall into place of their own accord once the fulcrums become visible. BILDT immediately grasps that it is about preventing total transformation. KUCKHAHN[23] improves the constant interpolation, 'said courage' by making it 'courage is supposed to have said'.[24]

In 1950, when the play was being re-rehearsed as a result of cast changes, the third-person method was further refined:

> am having some scenes transposed into the form of stories by the assistants, so that the actors can read their lines in the third person, with descriptive insertions. as they read they then do the moves and the main gestures. this clarifies the content and gait of the scene, and geschonneck, who is so excellent in the naturalistic mode, gets a feeling for the epic style for the first time and becomes 'transparent'.[25]

Transparency, an absence of actorly self-protectiveness, was important to Brecht. He had no wish to bamboozle an audience. On the contrary, the task of the actor was to draw the audience's attention to everything worth noticing. The poem 'Showing Has to be Shown' treats of this first item in Brecht's rehearsal manual:

> All attitudes must be based on the attitude of showing
> This is how to practise: before you show the way
> A man betrays someone, or is seized by jealousy
> Or concludes a deal, first look
> At the audience, as if you wished to say:
> 'Now take note, this man is now betraying someone and this is how
> he does it.

> This is what he is like when jealousy seizes him, and this
> Is how he deals when dealing.'[26]

Weigel's demonstration of Mother Courage's behaviour when dealing was a recurrent feature of her performance. Since dealing is an unspectacular activity, her epic task was to make it spectacular.

One typically concrete and specific way in which she did so was to insist on selecting her stage properties – the dealer's wares as well as items for mundane use around the camp – herself. In another poem, 'Weigel's Props', Brecht celebrates the exactness of her choice:

> Each item
> In her stock is hand picked: straps and belts
> Pewter boxes and ammunition pouches; hand picked too
> The chicken and the stick which at the end
> The old woman twists through the draw-rope.[27]

This is more than attention to detail; it is attention to meaning. In a play about material circumstances, matter matters. The selling, preparation and consumption of food, for example, is of great importance throughout the play. Because food signals a tension between need and desire, Brecht was always interested in the ways in which human beings treated it. Charles Laughton's gorging Galileo thrilled him, and of the film-director Jean Renoir, when he met him in Los Angeles, he noted: 'it is funny, almost exciting, to watch monsieur renoir eating a sausage. there is nothing wrong with *his* senses.'[28] Similarly, the 'theatrical elegance' (p. 350) with which Bildt, as the Cook, prepared the capon in Scene 2, making the preparation an expression of his erotic fantasies, was singled out by Brecht, who saw in it an example of implied performance. The Cook did *not* push home his courtship of Mother Courage *but* he caressed the capon. When, in Scene 9, this same Cook is reduced to begging for food and has to leave the stage to consume a bowl of thick soup, the ill effects of war are under special scrutiny. It was typical of the care with which stage furniture was selected for *Mother*

Courage that the makeshift table, at which Mother Courage, Kattrin, Swiss Cheese and the Chaplain eat their cramped, dejected meal after the Catholic raid in Scene 3, should draw attention to the act of eating. I was reminded of it when my reading of the play on a flight from Berlin to London was interrupted by the arrival of one of those prepacked meals that are the thin end of airline largesse. It is not only that the very idea of food is made strange on such occasions, but also that the act of eating it is rendered unlikely by the awkwardness of the implements and the circumstances. Seats too low, or tables at an awkward height, had a similar effect in *Mother Courage*. Even the act of sitting, which we take for granted, becomes noticeable when the stool is too high or one of its legs broken.

Such *Verfremdungseffekte*, often incursions of the openly theatrical into the secretive world of fiction, are always invitations to the audience to participate in the play's thinking. In Elizabeth Wright's provocative view, 'By means of a variety of disjunctive techniques and devices [Brecht] did his best to abandon dialogue in favour of discourse.'[29] It is properly with the audience that a consideration of the 1949 *Mother Courage* should end. There is, in the first place, the actual, historical audience and, in the second place, the 'new' audience Brecht hoped for and even, to some extent, anticipated.

Before the official première of *Mother Courage* on 11 January 1949, there was a closed performance for members of trade unions, a group of trainee Party officials and a large body of workers from the Hennigsdorf steelworks. The play lasted well over three hours. Even after the speeding up that is achieved when a production has run itself in, it remained unusually long. Act 1 (Scenes 1–7) took two hours and Act 2 a further hour. The change-over between scenes was unhurried, never less than fifty seconds and sometimes over ninety.[30] Even so, Brecht wrote,

> the workers from the hennigsdorf steelworks proved to be wonderful spectators. at first they sat like passers-by, watching from outside the

fence, from whom neither approval nor disapproval was required, but after the scene with the song of capitulation they clapped and then they interrupted the scene with the death of dumb kattrin with loud applause when she refuses to take the officer's word of honour. and at the end they forgot to jump up and dash for their coats, even though the play is a long one and the trams do not run late.[31]

In this first audience, Brecht believed, perhaps partly because he wished to believe, that he had found people for whom the interestingness of an actor was based 'on the interest he brings to the social phenomenon with which he is concerned in his acting'.[32] Elizabeth Wright considers 'utopian' this wish of Brecht's 'to produce an audience who would rejoice at the contradictions of a necessarily estranged world – the uncanniness of a world in flux, the constant shifting of figure and ground in a dialectical movement',[33] but she is in danger of creating the utopianism by her own choice of words. More simply, Brecht's project – not a unique one – was to create a form of theatre in which actors and audience participated jointly in the production of the text.

The critical reception of *Mother Courage* at the Deutsches Theater was warm, and the original run of the play was a sell-out. Plans for the formation of a permanent company were enhanced, but there were ominous signs as well. On 6 January 1949, five days before the première, Brecht was called out of rehearsal for a meeting with Friedrich Ebert, the Mayor of East Berlin, and the current Intendants of the Deutsches Theater and the Theater am Schiffbauerdamm: 'the mayor said neither hail nor farewell, didn't address me once and uttered only one sceptical sentence about dodgy projects which destroy things that are already in place'.[34] After the encounter, Brecht was for the first time 'conscious of the foetid breath of provincialism here'.[35] Mother Courage's failure to learn from her experiences in the play was not going to find favour with Communist Party officials, whose taste was for positive proletarian heroes in a climate of socialist realism. This was an issue on which Brecht was obdurate to the point of defiance. His ambiguous note on the reaction of trainee officials at the preview reads, 'the fact that courage, even in her greatest misery, learns nothing only aroused the pity of this audience'.[36] It is not clear from the German text whether this was a pity bordering on contempt or a pity tipping towards empathy, though the former seems more likely. It had been a first objective of the rehearsals to establish for Weigel a way of playing Mother Courage that would negate the audience's impulse to identify with her suffering motherhood:

> we have to alter the first scene of COURAGE, since it has in it the seeds
> of what enabled the audience at the zürich production to be moved
> mainly by the persistence and resilience of a being in torment (the
> eternal mother creature) – which is not really the point.[37]

The full text of the play in performance was to be produced by the interaction of character and audience on the theme of understanding; this was to be the new dialectical theatre 'of the man who has begun to help himself'.[38]

Until his encounter with Mayor Friedrich Ebert, Brecht had every reason to hope that his Marxist-Leninist views would be enthusiastically received in the new Marxist-Leninist state. Here at last he might find the 'viewer who produces the world' of whom he had written during his exile in Finland:

> it must not of course be a matter of handing out a patent solution
> to the riddle of the world to each member of the audience. only as a
> member of society is he in a position to take practical action. and
> the concept *praxis* gets a quite new, powerful meaning.[39]

Brecht was temperamentally disinclined to spoon-feed audiences, but he was determined to play fair by them. The sort of dramatic suspense that playwrights can achieve by the tactical withholding of information was alien to him. His audiences were to be fully informed. It was the business of rehearsal to put in place and to draw attention to everything that would enable the audience to sustain a rational dialogue with the play. That is not to deny Brecht's manifest designs on his audience. He was, as has already been suggested, a realist, but one who wished to present reality, not as recognisable, but as masterable. In this respect, *Mother Courage* proved problematic in performance. Even Weigel, and certainly Hurwicz, could not entirely overcome the theatregoer's 'deeply engrained habit . . . to pick out the more emotional utterances of the characters and overlook everything else' (p. 341). More inimical than that, though, was the general tendency to receive the play as a pacifist outcry against the natural phenomenon of war: 'regardless of all our efforts to represent the war as an aggregate of business deals, the discussions showed time and time again that people regarded it as a timeless abstraction' (p. 341). When the production toured Poland in 1953, it was warmly received by audiences but also attacked in many quarters for its political passivity. Forced to recognise that 'all this does not satisfy the impatience of our new socialist society',[40] Brecht took refuge in simplistic assertiveness:

> The proletarians in the audience, the members of a class which really can take action against war and eliminate it, must be given an insight – which of course is possible only if the play is performed in the right way – into the connection between war and commerce: the proletarian as a class can do away with war by doing away with capitalism.
>
> (*pp. 385–6*)

By the time Brecht wrote this (it was among notes published in 1956) he and the Ensemble were under near-continuous criticism from the ideologues of socialist realism. The honeymoon period lasted less than two years, although the generous subsidy was maintained in silent recognition of the propaganda benefits the company brought to the state.

Ironically, the focus of the attacks on Brecht was the work of Stanislavsky. The Moscow Art Theatre had become a model for the new age, and the Stanislavsky system was harnessed to the socialist-realist aesthetic. In the German Democratic Republic the impact was at its strongest between 1951 and 1953. On 4 March 1953 Brecht noted in his journal that 'our performances in berlin have almost no resonance any more'. A month later there was a Stanislavsky Conference at the East Berlin Academy of Arts. At it, according to Meg Mumford, 'more attention was given to establishing a Brecht–Stanislavski opposition and to anti-Brecht diatribe than to exploring Stanislavski's ideas'.[41] Although Weigel was the official spokesperson of the Ensemble, Brecht attended some sessions of the Conference, intervening at least once. He was not entirely without allies, but he was beleaguered and on the defensive throughout 1953. It is unsurprising, under the circumstances, that his response to the suppression of the workers' protest on 17 June 1953 was muted. It was a long way from the hopefulness of the opening night of *Mother Courage*, so delicately recorded in the poem 'For Helene Weigel':

> And now step in your easy way
> On to the old stage in our demolished city
> Full of patience, at the same time relentless,
> Showing what is right.
>
> What is foolish, with wisdom
> Hatred, with friendliness
> Where the house has collapsed
> What was wrong with the plans.
>
> But to the unteachable now show
> With some slight hope
> Your good face.[42]

The new theatre had an old audience, after all, most of them sharing the characteristics Brecht once ascribed to the 'bad member of a theatre audience':

> somebody who has too many and too exact views about what is coming at him. somebody who has too few and too vague notions about what he is hoping to react positively to. somebody who does

not allow himself to be influenced, either positively or negatively, by the mass of the public. somebody who is interested neither in the subject nor in the way it is treated.[43]

It was Brecht's own kind of courage that enabled him, albeit with lesser expectations, to continue with the Ensemble until his death in 1956.

CHAPTER FOUR

MOTHER COURAGE IN ENGLISH

There were two British productions of *Mother Courage* in 1955, when Brecht's name was not yet widely known in the English-speaking world. The earlier was an open reading at the Institute of Contemporary Arts, under the direction of the influential Marxist, Eric Capon. The second, unfashionably staged at the Taw and Torridge Festival in Barnstaple, was Joan Littlewood's production with the Theatre Workshop company. Neither the reading nor the production did much to advance the reputation of play or playwright. Kenneth Tynan, the only major newspaper critic to make the trip to Devon, disparagingly reported it to be 'a production in which discourtesy to a masterpiece borders on insult'.[1] Two months later, in August 1955, *Waiting for Godot* had its English première at the Arts Theatre in London. Most reviewers hated it, but its theatrical impact was irresistible. The combination of inscrutability and minimalism provided an extraordinary stimulus to a nation's theatre all too aware of its need for renewal. Beckett, not Brecht, was the revelation of 1955. Whilst seeming to do so little, *Waiting for Godot* implied so much. It was both philosophically sophisticated and politically innocent. Beyond the concrete sparseness of the staging he requires, Beckett has nothing in common with Brecht. A public that accommodated one might have been expected to have difficulty with the other.

It is only in retrospect that we can recognise the shifts in perception brought about by the work of the English Stage Company at the Royal Court Theatre. The excitement generated by John Osborne's *Look Back in Anger*, which opened in May 1956, probably eased the eventual passage to England of a political theatre, a passage that was certainly accelerated by the visit of the Berliner Ensemble later in the same year. But it would be some time before the English stage and its promoters were ready for a political drama that was both adult and home-grown. Joan Littlewood's production of *Mother Courage* took place a year too early to benefit from any whiplash effect of *Look Back in Anger*. It would probably not have benefited anyway. The production was not a happy one. Littlewood had met Brecht, liked him – the liking was mutual – and so had personal as well as political reasons for wishing to bring him to the attention of the British public. When Oscar Lewenstein visited Berlin on her behalf, Brecht readily granted performance rights. Littlewood could make use of the design for the Ensemble production and of Dessau's score, he volunteered; and he would, moreover, send Carl Weber, one of his young directors, to assist with the production. Both Lewenstein and Brecht were acting on the understanding that Littlewood herself would be playing the title role. That had, indeed, been her original plan; and it may be that an awareness of the scale of the double task of director and leading player lay behind Brecht's offer of Carl Weber. Or it may be that Weber was sent to make sure that things were done properly. Either way, Littlewood wanted none of it, and Weber found himself excluded from rehearsals. He had also to report back to Brecht that Littlewood was no longer playing Mother Courage. It was at this point that Brecht put his foot down – either Littlewood played the part or the rights would be withdrawn. Forced to learn the part in a hurry, and temperamentally ill-disposed to such authoritarianism (from outside the company, at least), Littlewood was ill-prepared and probably resentful. Her own stubborn survivalism put her in touch with an ambiguous aspect of the character she played, but she could neither sing the part nor, in the event, pace it. The fourteen-strong company that made the trip from Stratford East to Barnstaple met with the kind of cool reception that has been all too common in British productions of Brecht's plays.

The fairy-tale outcome of the Theatre Workshop production of *Mother Courage* would probably have been rave notices for Littlewood and a national tour. A socialist theatre ensemble would then have been responsible for forcing the British theatre establishment to take notice of Brecht. Such an outcome was unlikely from the start. It is perilous enough to undertake *Mother Courage* with a cast of only fourteen. To undertake it in the headlong fashion that was Littlewood's forte is to court disaster. Theatre Workshop rehearsals were explosive, volatile and, at best, inspirational, but they were not discursive. The atmosphere was more often confrontational than reflective – an extreme contrast to the slow and meticulous mode of rehearsal at the Berliner Ensemble, with their long pauses for discussion and the apparent detachment of the creator–director. *Mother Courage* is altogether too deliberate a play to benefit, in the normal way of Theatre Workshop productions, from Littlewood's interventionist theatricality. Given better conditions and more time, she might have made it work. She was, after all, a magnificent manipulator of improbable theatre. But she was at her best when working towards rather than from a text, certainly a text as monumental as that of *Mother Courage*. However, the Barnstaple performance did as little harm to Brecht's reputation as it did good. Very few people saw it, and the company decided not to maintain it in the repertoire. When I asked Joan Littlewood about it in December 1995 she ducked her head and said, 'Dreadful'. Her chief memory was of the nausea she suffered when plucking the long-dead chicken that was substituting for the capon in Scene 2. *Mother Courage* was the only Brecht play performed by Littlewood's Theatre Workshop, and it was much more the idea than the practice of Brecht and the Berliner Ensemble that permeated her work at Stratford East.

THE NATIONAL THEATRE AT THE OLD VIC, LONDON, 1965

The subsequent stage history of *Mother Courage* in Britain was radically affected in the late summer of 1956, when Brecht's own production was part of the Berliner Ensemble's season at the Palace Theatre in London. Kenneth Tynan's much-quoted review, magisterially delivered, aimed to leave the dithering commercial theatres of the English-speaking world with very little room for manoeuvre:

> [Brecht] wrote morality plays and directed them as such, and if we of the West End and Broadway find them as tiresome as religion, we are in a shrinking minority. There is a world elsewhere.[2]

The visit of the Ensemble was certainly timely. The English theatre was taking stock of itself in 1956, and unusually ready to look outwards for inspiration. But the evidence suggests that, whilst individual writers and directors were excited by what they saw of the Berliner Ensemble, the professional theatre at large was intimidated. George Devine directed Peggy Ashcroft in *The Good Woman of Setzuan* [*sic*] at the Royal Court in October 1956, but it was not until 1960, when Bernard Miles played Galileo at the Mermaid Theatre in London, that another major theatre attempted a Brecht production. William Gaskill recalled in 1965 that, 'for many of us working in the theatre [the Berliner Ensemble's *Mother Courage* was] the most important single production we have ever seen – the most influential',[3] but there is a deterrent element in excellence. Gaskill was speaking in the context of his own *Mother Courage*, staged by the National Theatre at the Old Vic nearly ten years after the visit of the Berliner Ensemble. In the interim there had been low-key productions at the Unity Theatre in London (1958), the Old Vic (1961) and the Merseyside Unity in Liverpool (1964). None of these was more than a pale shadow of the Berlin original, so that Gaskill's production for the National Theatre in 1965 promised to be the first major English staging.

The auguries were good. Gaskill was already the most Brechtian of English directors, with a well-received production of *The Caucasian Chalk Circle* (1962) already behind him. He was the most effective creator of an ensemble then working in the English theatre, and he was uniquely sympathetic, both politically and aesthetically, to Brecht's ideas. Writing in 1988, he again recalled the impact of the Berliner Ensemble's London season:

The first production we saw was *The Caucasian Chalk Circle* which was impressive and very beautiful to look at . . . But it was *Courage* that blew our minds. When the half-curtain whizzed back and we saw Helene Weigel smiling up at the sky, Angelika Hurwicz blowing into her harmonica and the cart pulled against the revolve by a sweaty, piggy-eyed Ekkehard Schall and tiny, timid Heinz Schubert we knew this was it. They seemed to affront the audience in the Palace Theatre with their sureness. Nothing was hidden, nothing secret. It looked wonderful.[4]

It may be that Gaskill was too much in awe of the Berliner Ensemble. It cut him off from the actors in the Royal Shakespeare Company, some of whom expressed their anxiety to Peter Hall at a late stage of the rehearsals for *The Caucasian Chalk Circle*. On that occasion Hall stepped in to pull the production together for opening night, although the substantial work was Gaskill's. It was in rehearsing towards the narrative of the play that he had learned the Brechtian trick of 'seeing a play as a series of actions governed by decisions'.[5] For the first time an English director was proposing to approach *Mother Courage* as Brecht himself had approached it. The outcome, though, was disappointing, as it has so often been since then. Among the attempts to account for the relative failure of Gaskill's production, Martin Esslin's is particularly plausible:

> . . . the English style of acting already being cooler and more
> Brechtian than Brecht's own company's, most of his polemics against
> the heavy German style (and that after all is what his insistence on
> non-identification and alienation is really concerned with) are totally
> inapplicable to English conditions. Not knowing this, and thinking
> that Brecht was attacking the style currently prevalent in England as
> well as in Germany, some directors made desperate attempts to cool
> their actors down even further. As a result, for example, William
> Gaskill's production of *Mother Courage* at the National Theatre (1965)
> achieved an effect tantamount to miniaturization of the play and its
> characters.[6]

As always when reading Esslin on Brecht, we have to be alert to the intrusiveness of Esslin's own agenda. He attempts constantly to call into doubt Brecht's political commitment – in this case by way of an almost comically disingenuous parenthesis – but the point about acting styles is not without substance. English actors, lacking an ideologically appropriate understanding and context, and textually deprived of a comforting refuge in psychology, have often played Brecht with a puzzled perfunctoriness. It is arguable that *Mother Courage* can be played to full effect only by a company that knows and shares Brecht's purposes. Such a company is not easily assembled in Britain. What Esslin records of Gaskill's production of *Mother Courage* – essentially a coolness towards the play – was recognised by Gaskill himself:

> . . . for the actors the play was just another play in the repertoire of the company; there was no common attitude, political or aesthetic in the work. I don't think that the Berliner Ensemble was made up of dedicated Marxists, but they were part of a team committed to left-wing plays . . . Obviously, we couldn't re-create those circumstances, but without some shared approach to the content of the play the theatrical experience is less.[7]

It is a problem that will generally confront directors whose period of rehearsal is limited. It takes time to persuade an actor to see the play as well as the part.

More to his surprise, Gaskill was made aware of another feature of *Mother Courage* – 'that even in Brecht you need stars'.[8] This was not something he had noticed when directing *The Caucasian Chalk Circle* three years earlier. His Grusha then had been Patsy Byrne and his Azdak Hugh Griffith. Byrne was an excellent company member, seen more often in secondary roles but with a well-proved talent for comedy timing. Griffith was a magnificent eccentric, never fully a star, though he might have become one if he had been better able to control his indulgence. With that experience behind him, Gaskill felt justified in casting *Mother Courage* from the company available at the National Theatre. Madge Ryan was more than competent, but she was not a star, and the role of Mother

Courage proved too big for her. That, at least, was the verdict of most reviewers at a time when Weigel was still remembered, and Gaskill came to feel, as subsequent British directors have generally felt, that the part of Mother Courage calls for that totality of possession of the stage that is the hallmark of the star actor. Kenneth Tynan had tried to persuade him to approach Anna Magnani, perhaps knowing that she had been tempted by the offer of the part in New York in 1962. A few years earlier the name of Gracie Fields had been mentioned in connection with the part, but by 1965 she had retired to Capri. Her involvement in *Mother Courage* would have radically altered the status of the songs. We should, perhaps, be grateful that no one proposed Vera Lynn.

THE SHADOW OF HELENE WEIGEL

The casting of Mother Courage, even for those who feel it ought not to be a problem, is certainly an issue which has clouded the reception of the play on the British stage. The authority of Weigel still intervenes, as is immediately apparent in the ten-line entry accorded her in *The Cambridge Guide to World Theatre* (1988):

> Austrian-born actress and theatre manager, who worked under Jessner and was Brecht's leading actress, becoming his second wife in 1928. Her performances in *The Mother* (1932) and *Mother Courage and her Children* (1949) gave the definitive interpretation of his female proletarian characters. The nominal director of the Berliner Ensemble, she took control of the company after Brecht's death and the tours she mounted established Brecht's international reputation.

The entry is embellished by a top-of-the-page photograph of Weigel's silent scream.[9] It is always easy to pick fights with reference works, since their necessary selectivity leads almost inevitably to distortion. What is instructive here is the re-enforcement of a notion of 'definitive interpretation' with a notorious visual image. On the nineteenth-century stage, the silent scream would have been accounted a 'point' and rewarded with rounds of applause. It was these points that became definitive; they were copied (and augmented) by successive performers of major roles. But definitive interpretations were not generally recognised until late in the Victorian era. On the contrary, it was precisely because Edmund Kean's Richard III was so remarkable that theatregoers clamoured to see Macready in the part. Two physically and vocally contrasting actors, each using many of the same points, attracted public interest and debate. It was only in indifferent plays that actors laid definitive claim to a part: Irving's Matthias in *The Bells* (1871) is the best-known example. The status of Weigel's Mother Courage, then, is an unusual one. Even now, in Britain, critics rarely review a performance without reference to it. The Lady Bracknell of Edith Evans is the closest parallel, but the parts are in no way comparable. The English theatre has had its great Hedda Gablers, but no definitive one, and an actress can play Shaw's Saint Joan or Shakespeare's Cleopatra without having to look over her shoulder at a particular precedent. Why does Weigel's Mother Courage cast so long a shadow?

The answer is not, of course, a straightforward one. It should, first of all, be acknowledged that Brecht is unusual among political playwrights in his delight in towering parts and dominating actors. The showmanship he had admired in Max Reinhardt was part of his own make-up too. Galileo and Mother Courage, Puntila and Shen Te, Schweyk and Azdak – even the early Baal, Galy Gay and Pelageya Vlassova – dictate, to an unusual degree, the conduct and impact of the plays in which they figure. Howard Brenton has referred to such of Brecht's plays as 'the spectacular show with the big main part at the centre'.[10] It is clear from all that he wrote about it that Brecht's admiration for working actors with star quality underwrote his strange partnership with Charles Laughton. Peter Lorre, Oskar Homolka, Elisabeth Bergner, Therese Giehse, Ernst Busch and, of course, Weigel were others who inspired in him uncharacteristically prolonged expressions of humility. What he particularly admired in actors was the ability to play a role in such a way as to demonstrate awareness of its social context and conditioning. Showmanship in the service of social comment was, for Brecht, the great actor's gift to the serious purposes of theatre. When friends in his Los Angeles circle complained of the unevenness and eclecticism of *Citizen Kane* he noted in his journal:

> i find that it is unfair to apply the word eclectic to techniques, and modern to use a variety of different styles for a variety of different functions. they are critical of orson welles's showmanship, but he shows things that are interesting from a social point of view, though it may be that as an actor he has not yet turned his showmanship into a stylistic element.[11]

Where showmanship was aligned with style, Brecht was ready to recognise the outline, at least, of epic acting – even where the content was without political bite. Having watched Laurette Taylor's startling comeback as Amanda in Tennessee Williams's *The Glass Menagerie*, he noted that 'her acting is epic'.[12] Unless Brecht also perceived an epic quality in the writing, this is curious evidence of his susceptibility to egregious performance. Laurette Taylor was an outsize personality, as, in a very different way, was Helene Weigel. It is all the more understandable, then, that British directors have sought out proven stars to play Mother Courage. But this, too often, has been to ignore the second quality essential to the playing of the part: an informed awareness of its political significance. Weigel's performance was underpinned by anger, her own rather than Mother Courage's. It is not often that successful British actresses carry that kind of anger. The choice of Flora Robson for the BBC television production in 1959 was implicitly a tempering of a bold piece of scheduling. Robson's capacity to represent endurance in the face of suffering had won her the part, and the whole production was designed to service that capacity. The play emerged as no more than a gentle stab at the political naivety of Macmillan's Britain.

Robson was pre-eminently a stage performer, and she was very obviously constrained by the restrictions of television drama in its fledgling years. Two decades later the stage reclaimed an actress who had become by then a larger-than-life television personality, when Peggy Mount played Mother Courage in Birmingham. Mount was a large woman, famous for her loud voice. The secret of her television appeal (above all as Ma Larkin) was that, although she played the harridan, no one believed that she was one. She had showmanship and personality, but no hunger and only the habitual pretence of anger.

THE ROYAL SHAKESPEARE COMPANY AT THE BARBICAN CENTRE, 1984

In the years between the television version and the 1978 performance in Birmingham, *Mother Courage* had been staged at most of Britain's major regional theatres as well as by Gaskill in London. The boldest of these productions, perhaps, was that directed by the young Alan Dossor for the Nottingham Playhouse in 1967. Against the British drift, Dossor's production was stridently political, set in the Vietnam War and openly anti-imperialistic. Gaskill's respect for the Berliner Ensemble had been evident in his approach to the play. He had not set out to imitate, but he had found nothing to improve on the economy and accuracy of Brecht's production, in which 'Every moment, every image, was honed down to its simplest and most meaningful statement; its effect was both political and aesthetic.'[13] Dossor's approach was consciously iconoclastic, but the political priorities were not distant from Brecht's own. When the Royal Shakespeare Company came to stage the play in 1984, the iconoclasm was altogether more oppositional. The songs (music by George Fenton, lyrics by Sue Davies) were incorporated into the flow of the action. *Verfremdung*, it had been decided, was irrelevant to the play. The commissioned 'translator', Hanif Kureishi, produced a version designed to turn 'a long, tedious, stodgy anti-war play' into something 'warm and funny'.[14] Most of the warmth was to be provided by an endearingly randy Mother Courage. Kureishi's version, then, constituted a direct challenge to Brecht's view of character as socially constructed, a challenge re-enforced by Howard Davies's direction and Judi Dench's performance. For Dench the part offered an escape from her customary stage gentility, but the escape was made at the expense of the politics. Her Mother Courage was the kind of person who, in the everyday world, is affectionately termed a 'character'. In order further to naturalise (and neutralise) the play, Davies and Kureishi smoothed the flow of the narrative, ensuring that the scenes were played, in direct contravention of Brecht's epic intention, 'one out of another' rather than 'one after another'. For the audience, most of whom must have been presuming that they were watching a play by Brecht, the end-product was reassuringly familiar. *Mother Courage* had been incorporated into the very Aristotelean tradition against which Brecht had set himself. Gerald Jacobs, in his hagiographic 'authorised biography' of Judi Dench, expresses a common response, one that was clearly encouraged by the whole treatment of the play in performance:

> In fact, the audience's sympathy is *needed* to make the play work dramatically. And the nightly ovations for Judi Dench constitute a loud declaration of sympathy. Her Mother Courage is not just a profiteer, but a caring parent; not a piece of political fabrication but a human being.[15]

Nor does it end there. 'Judi strode the stage', writes Jacobs, 'like a music-hall star. And, like the very best of music-hall stars, and *pace* Brecht, she expressed her character's foibles in basic human terms with which audiences can identify.' Jacobs is writing about Judi Dench, not Brecht – about whom his little learning is a dangerous thing. 'The play', he explains, 'is a long, well-modulated, anti-war harangue', but 'a sense of triumph at the production's close was not an irreverent sentiment, for this was an artistic triumph'. My impression is that Jacobs speaks for the majority of those who watched the play at the Barbican Centre. Confronted with what they feared to be an indigestible play, director and adaptor had set about making it more palatable. It is a disconcerting fact that, for the most part, they succeeded. As Christopher McCullough has observed, 'this operation was not offered to the public as a suppression of Brecht, but as a liberation of the true spirit of the artist from the thraldom of a political ideology'.[16] The British public was surprised to find that it liked Brecht after all. There were several cheers during the curtain-calls on the night I attended, and the atmosphere in the auditorium was warm and friendly. In the aftermath of the Falklands War, the play had a kind of topicality, but its triumphalism (or that of the production) seemed to me a direct contradiction of Brecht's intentions. Besides the many who applauded, there were those in the theatre who were very angry indeed. Nearly thirty years after Brecht's death, one of Britain's two leading theatre companies still considered it necessary to smuggle *Mother Courage* into London in disguise. There is, presumably, box-office evidence that the English do not like their theatre too political. If not, this kind of softening is merely wilful. If so, this kind of softening will do nothing to change attitudes.

THE GLASGOW CITIZENS' THEATRE, 1990

Approaches to Brecht in the English theatre have generally been based on the proposition that his work is difficult, that audiences will struggle with it, and that the necessary task is therefore one of alleviation. The Scottish experience, as represented by the Glasgow Citizens' Theatre, is different. There had already been four full-scale productions of Brecht at the Citizens' before 1969, when Giles Havergal and Philip Prowse assumed control of the artistic policy. Since then there have been nearly twenty. The theatre is in the once-notorious Gorbals district of the city, and it has been consistently responsive to an audience that it feels no need to patronise and no shame to inform. Hand-outs may carry details about unemployment, homelessness and inadequate housing in Glasgow, thus embedding the company's repertoire in a socio-political reality. The aim has been to establish an ensemble which combines a sense of locality with a confidence in its own idiosyncrasies. There have been two productions of *Mother Courage* at the Citizens'. The first, in 1970, was directed by Rob Walker, who was in no doubt about the play's political relevance but who decided to emphasise it by updating to World War II. The wagon was a war-battered truck mounted on ski-splints, and Ann Mitchell, part of a youthful ensemble, was an improbably young Mother Courage. Brecht's political stance was respected, but phrased with a strident theatricality – early evidence of the Havergal–Prowse signature – that embraced theatrical camp in the decision to have John Duttine play Yvette in drag. A provocative observation by Howard Brenton – one of whose full import I remain uncertain – is curiously apposite to Brecht at the Citizens':

> Brecht was fascinated with the sense of dignity which a great camp actor will always have. [Brenton has Charles Laughton in mind here.] They will always be on the back foot, in cricket terms, and will be oddly exploitative at great emotional moments. You think as a member of the audience: 'I must not weep or the actor will laugh at me'. Brecht liked this because he was after a story telling form of theatre.[17]

It is, I suppose, conceivable that the next British Mother Courage might be Simon Callow or Antony Sher rather than Fiona Shaw, Harriet Walter or Maggie Steed.

There was, though, an impelling logic in the choice of Glenda Jackson as the Citizens' Mother Courage in 1990. Jackson had just announced her intention to stand as a Labour candidate at the next General Election. Through all her virtuoso performances over the previous two decades, her hard intelligence had been her distinct quality – an associative history quite unlike Judi Dench's. The Citizens' production was scheduled as part of the Glasgow Mayfest.

It followed on the collapse of European communism and coincided with Glasgow's year as European City of Culture. Brecht's reputation was under new scrutiny in a context of capitalist triumphalism, an aspect of which continues to be a conscienceless celebration of the economic benefits derived from arms sales. Very soon Britain and the USA would go to war against Iraq in a campaign transparently linked to the command of oil. The star, the location and the timing of the 1990 *Mother Courage*, then, were peculiarly apposite, and it is not easy to account for the unexpectedly flat outcome. Margaret Eddershaw has noted a lack of political focus that allowed the impression that this was 'a play about the suffering caused by war rather than one about the immorality of trading off war', alerting us to the significant fact that 'the play had been three weeks into rehearsal before Glenda Jackson was given Mother Courage's purse'.[18] Eddershaw's sensitive observation of such carelessness about a crucial property is an admonitory contrast to Weigel's practice, but her description of the play as 'one about the immorality of trading off war' is too restrictive. A whole political system is on display, with war as its metaphorical clothing. The director, Philip Prowse, was perversely blind to that: 'I'm not a German. I'm not in a situation to set up a political discussion, unlike Brecht . . . I don't think it's as simple as whether you're a communist or not. It's to do with keeping trucking as an artist.'[19] Fortunately there was little evidence in the production that Prowse carried through this extraordinary appropriation of *Mother Courage* as a play about a durable artist dragging the wagon of aesthetic faith through hostile territory. On the contrary, Jackson sustained a quality of anger that merits comparison with Weigel's. But she was surprisingly willing to accept the depoliticisation of the text: 'My political interest in it is that it requires very much what I regard as a political basis – it's a team-play.'[20] Almost as much as Prowse's 'artistic trucking', this is meta-theatrical sentimentality. Jackson was an outsider in the ensemble, for many of whom the forcefulness of her personality was daunting. Her insistence that Kattrin's muteness should be absolute prevailed

Plate 4 Glenda Jackson confronts the recruiters in Scene 1 of the Glasgow Citizens' Theatre production, 1990, directed by Philip Prowse.

in rehearsal. There were to be none of the inarticulate sounds that Brecht had indicated since, in Jackson's view, Mother Courage's life-long project to make Kattrin invisible required, if it were to succeed, that she should be inaudible as well.[21] This is a serious suggestion, and it would be unfair to argue that Jackson made it because she was aware that Kattrin constitutes the most serious threat to Mother

Courage's dominant centrality; even so, a more dialectically aware director would have countered it. It was both a quality and defect of the production that Prowse was excited (over-excited?) by the projection of images of war. The intimate action was framed throughout by streams of anonymous refugees, displaced persons lacking Mother Courage's incentives. They were reminiscent of the figures who silently people Kozintsev's film of *King Lear*. I have no quarrel with the bleakness of the Citizens' *Mother Courage*, but some regrets at its squandering of opportunities.

In three respects this 1990 production was comparable with that at the Royal National Theatre in 1995. Firstly, Paul Dessau's score was abandoned entirely. It was replaced in Glasgow by hymn-tunes and in London by an original score. Secondly, and despite the availability of Ralph Manheim's excellent translation, both directors sought out versions by resident playwrights. Robert David MacDonald's picked out the street-wise emphases for Glenda Jackson, and David Hare's the witty pith for Diana Rigg, both betraying some anxiety about the capacity of the play to stand up for itself. The third link is stranger, and it requires a fuller description. Philip Prowse, who began his theatrical career as a designer and whose productions are visually rich, opened the performance with a striking image: a cornfield dotted with peasant reapers. It was an idyllic view of a Europe not yet devastated by the Thirty Years War. Once the idyll had been established, there was an explosion; the field vanished to leave the blackened walls and rubble that are the exemplary scenery of war. This rural idyll, as we shall see, reappeared in a new context at the National Theatre in 1995.

THE ROYAL NATIONAL THEATRE, 1995

The programme for the National Theatre's production included contributions from the composer, Jonathan Dove, and the adaptor,

David Hare. Dove offers a straightforward explanation for the abandonment of the Dessau score:

> Dessau's deliberately abrasive style must have been startling and invigorating to a contemporary audience, although when translated, the idiosyncratic word-setting can now produce the wrong kind of alienation.

Compared with Dessau's, Dove's score was gentle, even charming. Bullied by Brecht, Offenbach might have produced something similar. Such tunefulness is rooted outside the text – in a tradition that embraces light opera and the musical. The single reminiscence of the original score was the location of the musicians – in a box above stage-left. As at the Barbican and in Glasgow, an attempt was made (against Brechtian precedent) to incorporate the songs in the action. My impression is that this was not so much an aesthetic decision on the part of the director, Jonathan Kent, as it was a demonstration of his anxiety to keep up the pace of the production. He succeeded. The interval was placed, as it was in Brecht's production and as it generally is, after Scene 7, but the first half at the National lasted only ninety minutes and the second half under fifty. Hare's clever abbreviations helped. His was a slang-hungry version which cut linguistic corners rather than making any major cuts. His view of the play was advertised in a programme-note which also provides the Introduction to his published text. He sees Mother Courage as a naturally brilliant *petite bourgeoise* who fails to learn that lucidity is of no survival value in a war. Instead, she progresses towards silence: 'If I were to propose an alternative title for the play, it would be "The Silencing of Mother Courage".' The text does not fully bear out Hare's contention that Mother Courage says less and less as the play goes on. He is, perhaps, building too much out of her unique absence from Scene 11 and the brevity of Scene 12. But it is true that, as the narrative unfolds, Mother Courage finds herself with fewer and fewer people to say anything to. Brecht's dramaturgy makes one point; Hare's version sets out to make a significantly different one. His Mother Courage is the victim of an overwhelming phenomenon – war. Brecht set his sights on contradicting the view that war is an irresistible natural phenomenon. Hare's conclusion is a contradiction of Brecht's intentions:

> . . . two of the principal characters are . . . abstract nouns. They are Time and War. In their turn, they are attended by a flotilla of minor characters called Grief, Waste, Money, Religion and so on. One of the main jobs of a director approaching *Mother Courage* is to find a way of embodying Time and War, so he can show what they do to Mother Courage herself.[22]

For Hare, evidently, *Mother Courage* belongs to the genre of the Morality play, and Mother Courage herself is 'Everyperson'. Brecht would have considered this reading a malevolent distortion. His concern was not with the abstract but the concrete. War, he argued, is *not* an abstraction but concrete and man-made, and time, though a given circumstance, is subject to human intervention.

Perhaps under the influence of Hare, Jonathan Kent opened the production with a symbolic black bird of war, circling from the flies on a rotor arm and casting its ominous shadow on the upstage wall. The same bird continued its circle through each scene-break until I was heartily sick of it. Nor was this the only example of hyperbolic design. Paul Bond's background in opera was sometimes jarringly apparent. Through the first Act the design involved little more than the rapid technology of hydraulic lifts inside a circular revolving rim, with a scattering of furniture and props to change the scene. But the tall flats at the back of the Olivier stage could be raised to reveal alcoves. In Scene 4, for example, while Mother Courage sang her song of capitulation beside a comic little tent, the alcove upstage-left revealed an exquisite perspective model of the camp – with the wagon in place. That is entirely defensible, even witty, but the temptation of these upstage alcoves played havoc with Scenes 8 and 10. In Scene 8, when the onset of peace presages the ruin of Mother Courage and the death of Eilif, three of the upstage alcoves were filled with lines of beautiful autumnal trees, in receding

Plate 5 Diana Rigg as Mother Courage beneath the ominously circling bird of war in the Royal National Theatre production, 1995, directed by Jonathan Kent.

Hobbema-perspective. Evidently bypassed by war, they declared a permanence against which to measure the transitoriness of individual crisis. Designer and director were doing the job set for them by David Hare. They had embodied war in a black bird. Now they were embodying time in a visual image that bordered on kitsch. But it was in the treatment of Scene 10 that the production passed from the extravagant to the inexcusable. The year is 1635, and Mother Courage, having rejected the Cook's offer of a comfortable home in Utrecht, is harnessed next to Kattrin as they haul the wagon through the devastation of central Germany. An off-stage voice (in Brecht's text) lovingly sings of the joys of a small house and garden. In a fictional world Mother Courage could have had both. In the real world she has neither. In fact she has very little of anything. It is winter. In stage time, it is only a few minutes since she complained to the Cook (in Hare's version): 'In Wurtemburg I had a bag of salt, and all

I was offered was a plough. What good's a plough? Nothing grows any more, except thorns.' For what purpose, then, did Kent and Bond decide to have the Scene 10 song sung by three healthy women (as if freshly wardrobed by the D'Oyly Carte Company for a revival of *Patience*), standing knee-deep in corn-filled alcoves, with bobbing red poppies to match the red of their lips? Mother Courage and Kattrin were silhouetted spectres downstage of a triptych of pastoral plenty. Was the intention to provide the audience with some kind of reassurance that time is mightier than war? When Prowse employed the cornfield image in Glasgow he had a more serious point to make, and that point had nothing to do with Scene 10. Having seen the National Theatre production at its postponed first preview on 4 November 1995, I was confident that the setting for Scene 10 would have been changed before opening night, but it was still the same when I went again at the end of November. Its purpose remains mysterious to me, but its effect was nullifying.

Kent's production was built on a triangular 'character' principle, with the Cook and the Chaplain at either end of the base line and Mother Courage at the apex. The children were peripheral and the wagon a misjudgement. Michael Billington's description is depressingly apt:

> ... the cart itself is a bijou little tent on rubber wheels that has a nifty habit of rising and falling with the drum-revolve. It might do for a holiday in the Lake District but the one thing it never suggests is Courage's canteen-wagon and lifeline laden with the goods that keeps [*sic*] her going.[23]

The visual association was with an armoured truck of World-War-II vintage. I have no particular quarrel with the production's studied imprecision about its period setting, but there is no excusing two theatrical solecisms – the first, that any actor who was required to sit atop the truck displayed the precariousness of the perch (on both occasions that I saw the play, objects were dislodged and left lying on the stage); the second, that the outsize rubber tyres (with a deep tread that betokened newness) remained clean throughout. This carelessness about the play's most crucial property was surprisingly typical. The programme credits the National Theatre's Workshops for props and furniture. Under the circumstances the camouflage of anonymity was judicious. Mother Courage is a play about the material world, and a director who is indifferent to props should probably not undertake it.

The inconspicuousness of Lesley Sharpe's Kattrin was, I think, accidental. Her frantic circling of the wagon in Scene 3, when she was trying to alert her mother to Swiss Cheese's plight, was ineffective because, as was generally the case, Kent had too loose a hold on stage-groupings. The difficult Scene 5, a moment of confrontation between daughter and mother, lacked focus. The confrontation was missed because the dialectic was missed. Most surprising of all, Scene 11 – Kattrin's scene – was almost entirely without dramatic tension. The flown-in maze of unnecessary posts did nothing to help, and the lighting was far too dim. Perched on a high roof upstage-left, Kattrin was almost literally invisible. In trying to create realistic business for the incompetent soldiers, Kent lost the humour and obscured the pathos of the scene. He had not even noticed its aural qualities.

In theatrical terms, the performance sagged whenever Diana Rigg was not in control of it. There could be no clearer claim for the accuracy of Brenton's view that Brecht wrote spectacular shows with a big main part at their centre.[24] Rigg, whose sophisticated Emma Peel in the television *Avengers* had made her the cult figure of a generation, sought out the coarseness in the part of Mother Courage, conscious of the need to flout her own convention. Benedict Nightingale reported to readers of *The Times*:

> All along she was working so fiercely to turn her natural advantages to disadvantages. Her voice became a brassy blend of growl and snarl, her body took on a brash, truculent swagger. If I still could not quite credit her as a weather-flayed crone, I could certainly believe in her as an opportunist trader and canny survivor. She brings streetwise wit to

the stony roads of old Europe. David Hare's crisp, colloquial new
translation, with its 'she's winding me up' and its 'you dickhead', finds
more than the usual amount of humour in the play, and so does
Rigg.[25]

Nightingale's description of Hare's version is fair. The overriding
stylistic intention is to make the language as snappy as possible. Very
little is omitted, but the dialogue is shifted into a colloquialism that
enables actors to speak it faster. An exchange towards the end of
Scene 3, after Mother Courage has despatched Yvette to pay the
bribe that will save Swiss Cheese's life, may serve as an illustration.
In Manheim's translation it reads:

CHAPLAIN: I didn't mean to butt in, but what are we going to live on?
You've got an unemployable daughter on your hands.
COURAGE: You muddlehead, I'm counting on the regimental cashbox.
They'll allow for his expenses, won't they?
CHAPLAIN: But will she handle it right?
COURAGE: It's in her own interest. If I spend her two hundred, she gets the
wagon. She's mighty keen on it, how long can she expect to hold on to
her colonel? Kattrin, you scour the knives, use pumice. And you, don't
stand around like Jesus on the Mount of Olives, bestir yourself, wash
those glasses, we're expecting at least fifty for dinner.[26]

Hare provides a patina of slang and sharpens the impact:

CHAPLAIN: It's none of my business, but how are we going to survive? You
can hardly put your daughter to work.
COURAGE: I'm counting on the cash box, idiot. If we get to keep the cash
box, we won't be down on the deal.
CHAPLAIN: Are you sure Yvette's up to all this?
COURAGE: Why not? It's in her own interest. She thinks I won't be able to
pay her back and that way she'll get her hands on the cart. Colonels
don't last for ever. Kattrin, knives. There's the stone. And you, stop
standing around like Jesus having twins. Get on with it, wash the
glasses, there's at least fifty cavalry in tonight.[27]

Although (perhaps because) it means very little, 'standing around like Jesus having twins' earned a resounding audience-laugh, some of which was owed to David Bradley's feckless passivity as the Chaplain.

Rigg's Mother Courage relished her role as sex-object in the struggle between Chaplain and Cook. Left alone with the Cook in Scene 8, while the Chaplain is preparing to greet the peace by donning his discarded clerical gown, she played sexual variations on the notion of steadiness – and Hare was at pains to help. Where Manheim accurately translated Courage's 'I've only lived with one steady man, thank the Lord. I never had to work so hard', Hare substituted, 'I've only been with one steady man, thank God. I've never been so bored in my life'; and the point was forced home when Rigg ended the exchange with a bawdy laugh after her line, 'Don't say you've been dreaming of my toughness.' The laugh transformed the word 'toughness' into a euphemism for a previously shared secret part of her body. At moments like these – and there were several – Mother Courage's sexuality was personalised, taken outside the play's world of material transactions. The splendour was Rigg's rather than Brecht's.

Once again, and all too typically, a British director had chosen to side-step the challenge posed by *Mother Courage*. My performance notes record an audience snigger when, for the only time, Mother Courage cursed the war. Was it because Hare had changed the line to 'Damn the fucking war!'? For Billington, making the inevitable comparison, it was 'miles away from the weary, mournful shrug with which the great Helene Weigel uttered the line'. Rigg was possibly the best Mother Courage I have seen on the English stage, but this production was lightweight. It told a story but ran away from the story's meaning. With particular reference to the Royal Shakespeare Company's 1984 production, Maarten Van Dijk has written a cogent critique of anglophone presentations of Brecht's plays. The questions he asks are equally applicable to the National Theatre's production a decade later:

> What is the block so many Anglophone directors have about Brecht? Why do they seem to block his intentions in their work? Why are they

so reluctant to learn from a carefully worked out practice that could
be useful to any director in blocking a play? Why does the blocking of
the characters in a production of a play by Brecht nearly always lack
the realism and story-telling clarity of the famous photographs of
the models?[28]

The questions remain pertinent despite Van Dijk's apparent una-
wareness of the confusion that may be caused by his use of the same
verb (block) in two different senses. The answer to the questions
might expose the egotism or intellectual laziness of directors as well
as the unwillingness of anglophone theatre to accommodate theory.
For Roland Barthes, Brecht's formulation of social *Gestus* was one of
the clearest and most intelligent concepts in the whole body of dramatic theory.[29] It could surely be a starting-point for any rehearsal of
Mother Courage, but it is rarely there that British actors start. Glenda
Jackson's acknowledged starting-point for her performance was
Ethel Merman[30] – Lotte Lenya had told her that Helene Weigel, on
meeting Merman, had dubbed her 'Mother Courage'. (Interestingly,
my performance-jotting on Diana Rigg's singing of her song of war
in Scene 7 was 'Ethel Merman!'.) The show must, to be sure, go on,
but Ethel Merman is not a dramatic theory.

The director who plans a production of *Mother Courage* at the
end of the twentieth century is confronted with a dilemma. On the
one hand there is the challenge to understand and respect the text's
implicit ideology, already lucid but also re-enforced by the Model
Book and the film of the Berliner Ensemble's production; on the
other is the challenge expressed in Elizabeth Wright's adroit redirec-
tion of a famous Marxian dictum: 'The critics have merely inter-
preted Brecht in various ways, the point now is to change him.'[31]
But you cannot change what you do not understand; you can merely
circumvent it, as Davies did at the Barbican Centre and Kent at the
National Theatre. This was a point forcefully made by Barthes as
long ago as 1956:

> Certainly, Brecht's theatre is meant to be performed. But before per-
> forming it or seeing it performed, there is no law which says it must

not be understood . . . There is in the theatre of Brecht a precise ideological content, a coherent, consistent, remarkably *organized*, one which argues against abusive deformations.[32]

Barthes even makes the would-be director's job easier by picking out what he calls the main elements of Brecht's ideology:

> . . . the historical character and not the 'natural' one of human misfortune, the spiritual contagion of economic alienation, whose final effect is to blind to the causes of their servitude those same people it oppresses, the changeable order of Nature, the manipulability of the world, the necessary equation of means and situations (for example, in a rotten society right can only be re-established through a flippant judge), the transformation of ancient psychological 'conflicts' into historical contradictions, submitted as such to the correcting power of men.[33]

The writing (and rewriting) and Berlin staging of *Mother Courage* were designed to express these meanings, and Brecht's anxiety about false receptions of the play is worthy of respect. It is a text that fundamentally contradicts any belief (all too fashionable in Thatcherite Britain) in the naturalness of self-aggrandisement, and its ideology, whatever may be said by capitalist apologists, has not been proved wrong by the collapse of Soviet-style communism. On the contrary, at a time when Europe is once again being re-constructed, *Mother Courage* poses with renewed urgency its historical questions. The wry observation of Heiner Müller, artistic director of the Berliner Ensemble at the time of his death in 1995, is apposite here:

> It is a privilege for a writer to have experienced the end of three states: the Weimar Republic, the fascist state and the GDR. I don't suppose I'll live long enough to see the end of the Federal Republic.[34]

British directors, perhaps driven by the demand for the appearance of originality, have consistently fallen short in their understanding of *Mother Courage*, subjecting the play as a result to the 'abusive deformations' against which Barthes warned.

This is not an argument for slavish adherence to the Model, but it is an argument for appropriate preparation. At the heart of Brecht's enterprise was a determination to engage drama in the semantic struggles of twentieth-century art. It was a determination that he expressed variously in his plays, his poetry and his voluminous attempts at theoretical formulation. It is not unreasonable to expect a director of his plays to be well acquainted with Brecht's intelligence. It is a peculiarity of British theatre, though, that its directors are uneasy about relying too openly on their own intelligence. British actors, if they call a director an 'intellectual', are more likely to be intending an insult than a compliment; and if a director were to profess an academic interest in drama, he would be taking a risk with his career. This is less true in the USA, and two of the most thoughtful anglophone productions of *Mother Courage* owe their inspiration to prominent academics, Herbert Blau and Richard Schechner.

THE ACTOR'S WORKSHOP AT THE MARINES' MEMORIAL THEATRE, SAN FRANCISCO, 1956

Blau was the joint-founder of The Actor's Workshop in San Francisco. His *Mother Courage*, the company's twenty-second production, was the play's American première. It opened on 17 January 1956 in the Marines' Memorial Theatre, and it was a hostile review in the *San Francisco Chronicle* that sparked off a controversy during which Blau laid bare his passionate commitment to a theatre that participates in the politics of its own place and time. This was the period of the 'San Francisco Renaissance', when the city was the end of the trail for the fearsomely articulate Beat Generation. *Waiting for Godot*, which The Actor's Workshop famously toured to San Quentin Penitentiary in 1957, was the Beats' play, and its production in San Francisco brought the company its national reputation. But, according to Blau, it was the earlier work on *Mother Courage* that gave him and the actors the sense that 'what we did on stage was a moral commitment'.[35] During his twelve years with The Actor's Workshop, Blau fuelled his fierce idealism with anger about American policies at home and abroad. His landmark book *The Impossible Theater*, an extended manifesto, was published in 1964, shortly before Blau left San Francisco to take up an appointment at the Lincoln Center in New York. The manifesto finds its inspiration in the American Little Theatre movement and much of its intellectual rigour in the writings of Brecht:

> What we have been trying to develop in our theater is a counter-atmosphere in which the special properties of the dramatic form, devoted to crisis, are enlisted against the epidemic of mystifications.[36]

The account of *Mother Courage* that Blau provides is very much a retrospect. Significantly, seven years after directing *Mother Courage*, he had taken a less reverential approach to *The Life of Galileo*, and he now felt the need to speculate on the proposition that reverence for Brecht may be an impediment to the effective performance of his plays. He had visited Berlin in the meanwhile, and had taken note of the Ensemble's unstrained application of *Verfremdung*:

> What American acting has little sense of is the thing that astonishes you in the acting of, say, Ekkehard Schall, the young, crew-cut, intensely Communist Marlon Brando of the Ensemble, who played Arturo Ui. He is a political actor. And it is really eye-opening to see somebody get so much out of himself by force of *external* conviction.[37]

The American Method's privileging of *internal* conviction – when directing plays in the USA I have sometimes found the actors' hunger for motivation bulemic in its intensity – was an initial barrier to progress on *Mother Courage*. Blau records an occasion when the happy naivety ('in the best sense') of the company was dispersed into a feeling of terrible isolation:

> . . . our ardor, momentarily dampened, was revived more realistically when I said the production had to contain the knowledge that we were, after all, but a minority group in a minority form in a country

pledged to the protection of minorities, in a period in which they needed such protection.[38]

The sense of isolation had been precipitated by a sudden thunderstorm – a critical intervention by unstoppable Nature into a world that the rehearsing actors were just beginning to believe might be changeable.

The production of *Mother Courage* was little noticed outside San Francisco, and even within the city there was insufficient interest to sustain a long run. Blau reluctantly agreed to stave off financial disaster by reviving Arthur Miller's *The Crucible*, a play which, for him, 'lacked the terrifying impartiality of greater drama'.[39] Among the greater drama whose terrifying impartiality he was here identifying was *Mother Courage* – 'a revolutionary play, precisely because it can't be appropriated without misgivings by any particular cause'. There are conflicting views about the quality of Blau's production, but *The Impossible Theater* demonstrates how thoroughly his thinking had earned him the right to direct it. Through an encounter with the text, he had come to realise the need to develop stage-groupings that were, in themselves, signs, and the further need for those signs to invite a judgement from the audience. It was a discovery shared by the whole company when they came to work on Scene 5, the scene in which Mother Courage fails to prevent the Chaplain from commandeering her officers' shirts for bandages. It took them hours, says Blau, to work out the significant detail of an episode that lasts scarcely more than a minute in performance.[40] Such scrupulous attention to the articulation of stage-narrative is admirable. It enabled Blau and the actors to appreciate, through an exemplary quest for the appropriate *Gestus*, the constantly signifying on-stage activity of a play whose action (in the Aristotelean sense) is, for most of the time, in repose: '*Mother Courage* was the first of our plays to force us to reconsider the question of Time in the theater, the way it is passed, and the way it gives identity to Action.'[41] Time here is not the abstraction to which David Hare refers, but the concrete entity which, in the theatre, conditions the relationship between audience and actors; and the recognition of constant activity beyond the evident requirements of the narrative demonstrates the alertness of the rehearsal process. Barthes drew attention to this Brechtian characteristic in 1971, when he commented on the presence, along-side the written words of Brecht's text, of an autonomous language of setting and action.[42] It is to Blau's credit that he stumbled, through interrogative rehearsal, on a feature that has subsequently become the pleasure-ground of semioticians. For Barthes, whose insights gave such impetus to later semioticians, Brecht was 'a Marxist who has reflected on the value of signs: quite a rarity'.[43]

I make the assumption that The Actor's Workshop used Eric Bentley's translation of *Mother Courage* (as did the English National Theatre in 1965), but Blau does not make any comment on the fitting of the words to Dessau's score, which was used almost in its entirety. He records that the only song sung without *Verfremdung* was Mother Courage's lullaby over her dead daughter. The Chaplain's *Horenlied*, absent from Bentley's translation, was trans-posed to Scene 8 for reasons that Blau explains:

> I understand the principle of interruption, but in Scene 3 it seemed arbitrary, the only song sung when the focus was not in some way on the person singing. Performance bore out our choice; the song felt relevant (but still detached) and provided an excellent contrast to the burlesque scene which follows, in which Yvette discovers Peter Piper as the Cook.[44]

It is an explanation that falls short of justification. As I have already suggested, the *Horenlied* stands in ambiguous relationship with the death of Swiss Cheese. To transfer it to Scene 8 is to sacrifice that ambiguity. But this is a minor blemish in an admirable endeavour – part of The Actor's Workshop's attempt to put the American theatre back into touch with 'anything that really counts'.[45] It was, I am sure, no conscious imitation of Brecht on Blau's part to cast his wife as Mother Courage, and I know no more of Beatrice Manley's quality than the description of her in a reference work as 'a character actress known for her *hauteur* and technical control'.[46] It was Blau's belief that, at the end of the play, 'Brecht's desire for social change is figured in an image of hopeless changelessness'. He rejected the idea of a Mother Courage who squares her shoulders and looks steadfastly into the future as she hauls her wagon back to war:

> The stage, made to feel more emptily infinite by the disappearance of other properties (property?), becomes an existential platform. And Mother Courage pulling her wagon, alone against a hostile universe, resembles nobody so much as Sisyphus rolling his stone up the mountain, but with no residue of heroism.[47]

Blau's Brecht, in the culturally bleak America of the post-war era, has resonances of Albert Camus.

It would seem that Cheryl Crawford, a New York producer famous as one of the founders of the Group Theatre, was unaware of the San Francisco performance of *Mother Courage*. She writes in her autobiography (1977) of events in 1961:

> I saw several productions of the Berliner Ensemble and had tea with Helena [*sic*] Weigel, Brecht's wife, in the actors' canteen, where we talked about *Mother Courage*, which I had decided I must put on: I would give it its first American production.[48]

New York was then as ignorant as a dying dowager of life in the west wing. The first outcome of Crawford's determination to promote Brecht in New York was a production of George Tabori's revue anthology *Brecht on Brecht*. Starring Lotte Lenya,and including in its six-strong cast Tabori's Swedish wife Viveca Lindfors, the revue was a success in New York and on tour. Encouraged, Crawford entered into negotiations for a Broadway production of *Mother Courage*. Her director and co-producer, better known for his choreography, was Jerome Robbins. They read the play as the story of a heroic survivor, and Crawford evidently considered it an outline in need of some psychological filling, with characters 'like line drawings that need to be fleshed out'.[49] She offered the part of Mother Courage to Anna Magnani, a sultry Italian actress whose ability to combine the role of earth-mother with that of sexual pirate had been triumphantly displayed in Tennessee Williams's *The Rose Tattoo*, filmed in Hollywood in 1955. In the event Magnani turned down the offer, and the thirty-one-year-old Anne Bancroft gave an admired performance as a decidedly fiery opportunist. Broadway costs are so high that, despite takings of $29,000 per week, the play closed after less than three months early in 1963. *Mother Courage* is not a Broadway play – or a West End one – but it remained of interest to two of the initiators of *Brecht on Brecht*. In 1966 Tabori and Viveca Lindfors included it with Strindberg's *Dance of Death* in the repertoire of their five-person touring company, The Strolling Players: a typical episode in the split life of an actress who played trivial sex in Hollywood and classic roles on the American and Swedish stages. Lotte Lenya, the star of *Brecht on Brecht*, was drawn to the part of Mother Courage too. Not only did she return to Germany to play it in Recklinghausen in 1965, but she also played it in English in 1971 – as the only professional actor among students on the Irvine campus of the University of California. She was seventy-three at the time of her Californian performance, and her Mother Courage was inappropriately gentle.

THE PERFORMANCE GROUP AT THE PERFORMING GARAGE, NEW YORK, 1975

New York hosted two further productions of *Mother Courage* during the 1970s. The later of these was a radical adaptation rather than a translation. As part of the 1979/80 season, the New York Shakespeare Festival staged Ntozake Shangé's arrangement of Brecht's play for a black cast. Mother Courage was a former slave and the events occurred just after the end of the American Civil War. This was essentially a new play, inspired by Brecht but focused on racism in North America. Its place in the stage history of *Mother Courage* is marginal. It is with the production by The Performance Group, under the direction of Richard Schechner, that this chapter must finally concern itself: not because it was less radical in its approach to the material than Shangé, but because the text used remained Brecht's. The adaptation was environmental. The play was made to accommodate Schechner's ideas about the ritual nature of the theatrical transaction, and the nature of the playing space was allowed to determine the nature of the playing. As Barthes might have said, it was the autonomous language of setting and action that was adapted – the 'stage writing' – whilst the text remained about as close to the original as a translation can hope to be.[50]

Whilst Jerome Robbins had five weeks to prepare *Mother Courage* for Broadway, The Performance Group worked on their version for almost a year. Most of the rehearsals in the Performing Garage on Wooster Street were open, with up to forty people in casual attendance. For Schechner, 'their presence made a deep difference: work on the play began to include a public social core; and the work became about showing a way of working'.[51] Elements of incidental presence, 'a subtle infiltration of . . . everyday lives into the dramatic reality of the performance',[52] were retained after the formal opening in February 1975. When not required in the playing space, the actors were encouraged to remain visible in the makeshift 'green-room' area – relaxing, reading or merely sitting. As the audience arrived, actors might be changing into costume, warming up, checking props – nothing so intense that they could not break off to chat with old acquaintances or to make new ones. Schechner sat behind a cash-register selling tickets. The same cash-register would later be used by Mother Courage whenever she completed a deal, and its bell was rung whenever there was mention of money in the dialogue. The performance space was defined by irregular scaffolding on which the audience could sit (they could stand or sit on the floor as well), and the precise shape of the space could be changed at will by an arrangement of ropes secured to walls or to the scaffolds. The wagon was a stationary structure, also built of scaffolding and with a

Plate 6 The audience is scattered around the playing area of the Performing Garage at the opening of Richard Schechner's 1975 production with The Performance Group.

raised floor-level and a permanent set of steps. To 'pull' it, the actors simply donned a harness whose ropes might be held by the 'driving' Mother Courage or simply attached to the scaffold. Importantly (and inventively) the complex system of ropes and pulleys that dominated the environment was used to figure the deaths of the three children. Thus, while Mother Courage haggled with Yvette over the ransom money for her honest son, Swiss Cheese was suspended above the playing area. When he was shot, his body abruptly dropped a few feet towards the floor, to which it was subsequently lowered in preparation for Mother Courage's denial. In Scene 11 Kattrin worked a pulley to haul the ladder out of reach of her would-be assailants. When it was horizontal, about twelve feet above the floor, she perched on it to beat the drum. Paul Ryder Ryan's graphic description of her subsequent action gives some impression of its effect on an audience:

She then attaches a rope to a harness she is wearing and begins to drum. Finally, after unsuccessfully ordering her to stop the drumming, the Lieutenant orders her to be shot. A loud explosion from the Sergeant's gun fills the space. Kattrin pitches violently out of the ladder and hangs in space, one red boot still touching the ladder in an awkward split, smoke from the gun enveloping her body. She then is lowered to the ground, where Mother Courage, after a brief lamenting lullaby, strips her daughter down to her underwear so that she can sell the clothes.[53]

There are telling interpretations here – the wearing of the boots and the mercenary stripping. The first speaks to Kattrin's state of mind and the second to the state of Mother Courage's pocket.

The play was performed by nine actors – using Manheim's translation which had been the unanimous choice of the cast. The score was Dessau's, arranged by Alexandra Ivanoff, but Schechner made his own versions of the songs, abandoning any attempt at rhyme 'because to rhyme in English means that very often we just add words and ideas, staying away from the German because it is too complicated'.[54] There was no orchestra: instead, the instruments – three flutes, a violin, a viola, clarinet, concertina, piano, banjo, bugle, small cymbals, drum and tom-tom – were played by the actors. Joan MacIntosh was an undisguisedly young Mother Courage, Spalding Gray a boy-scout Swiss Cheese, Eilif a recognisably American paratrooper. In Schechner's view, not necessarily that of the audience:

> We didn't set the play in the 17th century, but we didn't modernize it either. The costumes were emblems of class. The garage was a place where theatrical, social, and economic transactions occurred.[55]

The attitude towards performance was well represented by Elizabeth Lecompte's playing of the Swedish General. She wore a moustache as a sign of masculinity but made no attempt physically or vocally to disguise her femininity: this was not caricature but straightforward indication of function.

The whole performance lasted four hours, but that included a significant interval after Scene 3. As this long scene progresses, Mother Courage, Kattrin and the Chaplain are preparing provisions for the Catholic army. In the Performing Garage, Joan MacIntosh, Leeny Sack (Kattrin) and Stephen Borst (the Chaplain) were preparing food for the audience, who could queue up to purchase supper – the cash-register again – during the interval. With a wry hint at cannibalism, Swiss Cheese was on the menu, but the occasion was essentially communal; a sharing between actors, technicians and spectators. Mother Courage sang her song of capitulation as the meal drew to an end. The rest of Scene 4 was cut and the play restarted in reduced light with the short and densely busy Scene 5. After eating with the actors, the audience found their relationship with them necessarily changed: it would be further adjusted during the playing of Scenes 9 and 10. For these cold and dismal scenes of penury, the doors of the Performing Garage were opened and the actors performed on the sidewalk of Wooster Street to a background of traffic and pedestrians. The spectators had to move out if they were to see what was going on. Even during the winter performances the Garage doors were left open for the rest of the play: 'Certain aspects of the cruel experience of Courage and her family were convincingly shared with the chilly audience.'[56]

It has always been part of Schechner's intellectual resourcefulness to be wise after the event. He could explain the replacement of the wagon by a stationary scaffold, for example, by recording the American association of wagons with the inappropriately purposeful passage of pioneers towards a predetermined goal. In more insistent retrospect, he placed this production of *Mother Courage* in the spectrum of his anthropological researches:

> By having open rehearsals, by opening the Garage door, by serving supper as part of the performance, *Mother Courage* was treated as a drama nested in a larger performance event. The ideas behind TPG's production of *Courage* are common in ritual performances: to control, arrange, or manipulate the whole world of the performance, not just

present the drama at its center. In this way a theatrical event in SoHo, New York City, was nudged a little way from the entertainment end of the continuum toward efficacy. Without diminishing its theatricality, The Performance Group worked to enhance Courage's ritual aspects.[57]

But that is to forget the production's contemporary reference to the Vietnam War. On 8 May 1975, instead of a scheduled performance of *Mother Courage* at the University of Michigan, Schechner and The Performance Group involved students and staff in 'an interpretation of The Thirty Years' War in Indochina in an attempt to display the impact of the war on the peoples of Vietnam and the United States'.[58] The Grand Ballroom of the Union Building was converted into a kind of fairground, with scaffolds, booth-stages and open playing areas. Various activities took place over the evening: a Vietnamese village was constructed (it would be destroyed at the end by people dressed as American soldiers); a tableau of photographs of the Kent State shootings was set up (in the finale Schechner placed animal offal on actors representing the slaughtered victims of both that shameful civil action and the Vietnam War); prisoners of war walked in aimless circles throughout whilst members of the audience were encouraged to dance to popular tunes of post-1945 America; a patriotic melodrama in support of the war was performed several times on a booth-stage in one corner of the room. The reference back to the cancelled production of *Mother Courage* was inescapable. As Schechner said at the time:

> It's an illusion that war industry helps. If you build a tank and send it away, you have to mine more. Basically, the raw materials come from the under-developed world. They get processed in the developed world and they get shipped again. In the process of that exchange, the very rich get richer. The poor, of course, get poorer, but that's acknowledged. What this play is about is that the middle class also gets ground down in the long run. And I think that this is a play, almost more than any Brecht play, directly addressed to the small

business man, to the small business person, I should say, because it's a woman. That's one prophecy we'd like to leave with this play.[59]

In the American context, it suddenly seems a comparatively short distance from *Mother Courage* to Arthur Miller's *Death of a Salesman*.

CHAPTER FIVE

MOTHER COURAGE IN THE GERMANIES AND IN FRANCE

The story of *Mother Courage* in the German-speaking theatre has shadowed the politics of division. It was in the war-torn Europe of 1941 that the play was first staged: in the city of Zürich in neutral Switzerland. And the part of Mother Courage – something that is often overlooked – was created by Therese Giehse. It is an accidental injustice of history that this major actress has surrendered her priority to Helene Weigel. Among those who saw both women in the part, Donald Soule has written a particularly suggestive comparison:

> My recollection of Weigel is that she couldn't help being heroic in some way or other (perhaps in nearly everything she did?). Does this kind of thing spring out of the actor's own personality – I suppose so. And in the case of women in our culture, does it not also spring out of their awareness of how they are thought to LOOK to men? Weigel was a handsome woman (I was struck meeting her in 1960 by this fact – and that she knew it). I find it difficult not to believe that Brecht's comparative judgements of the two women in the role – in any role – may have had some element of sexual awareness in it. Certainly, Weigel throughout her performance was always – even somehow suggestively at the end – aware of MOVING well and LOOKING good; see, for example, those photos of her STRIDING, waving, whatever. Weigel's suffering always, for me at least, seemed to have a bit of the 'noble' in it (always Antigone?).
>
> Giehse, of course, was not beautiful and was built like a dumpling with the face of a basset hound. Not a sexually attractive woman. Thank God. Nothing heroic about her Mother Courage. She was ordinary, sly, sometimes sour. Perhaps too funny at first? Can't

quite remember. Also the voice: not beautiful at all: can't remember the singing (did she at all?) – but the speaking voice was very ordinary, whereas Weigel's was strong and more assertive.

The parallel that is for me at least expressive of my very subjective recollections of the two actresses playing the same role: Weigel like Olivier, Giehse like Richardson.[1]

Whilst Brecht remained loyal to Weigel, it is clear that he revised his initially unfavourable impression of Giehse's Mother Courage. When Leopold Lindtberg first directed the play, Brecht was in Finland. With only the text to guide him, it is unsurprising that, in 1941, Lindtberg felt only the anti-war pulse of the play and led Giehse into a performance that was celebrated for its portrayal of endurance in the face of intolerable loss. It was his reading of reviews of his 'Niobe tragedy' in the Zürich press that led Brecht to make changes for the Berlin production. But Giehse was not a soft actress. Working with her for the Munich production of 1950, Brecht reported to Elisabeth Hauptmann: 'Rehearsals are going well. Giehse is wonderful, a tough businesswoman';[2] and he noted in his journal, after the Munich opening in October 1950, 'giehse is quite admirable in the way she completely revamps the moves she had used with such success in zürich and vienna'.[3] Munich provided Brecht with his first opportunity to experiment with the use of the Model: 'the moves based on the model are triumphant', he recorded and the whole production was 'quite different from berlin and excellent'.[4] The staging, that is to say, was as close to the Berlin Model as possible, but the effect was as different as the cast. Giehse was earthbound, immovable in contrast to the volatile Weigel, but they shared the 'epic' capacity simultaneously to criticise and to embody.

The Munich performance was exceptional in the early years of the divided Germany. Brecht's decision to remain in the Democratic Republic led to a virtual boycott of his plays in the Federal Republic. Until well into the 1960s it was only in Frankfurt, where the maverick Harry Buckwitz was Intendant of the Städtischen Bühnen, that the boycott was regularly broken. Even in Vienna the decision to stage *Mother Courage* in 1963 was taken with trepidation, and only after the Intendant of the Volkstheater, Leon Epp, had secured the agreement of the Austrian President. It was the first of a sequence of Brecht's plays at the Volkstheater, all directed by Gustav Manker, whose reputation as an outspoken intellectual provided Epp with some protection from his anti-communist critics. Manker's chosen Mother Courage was Dorothea Neff, an actress who had made her reputation in classic roles, and who, by 1963, was almost totally blind. The choice was partly a diplomatic one. Neff had actively assisted Jews to escape through Vienna during the Nazi occupation, and the Austrian government had subsequently rewarded her for her gallantry. It was Neff's overwhelming personality more than her performance that softened the Viennese reviewers – even those who considered the production of a play by Brecht an outrage. It is impossible to know how much the warmth of the critical response owed to the knowledge that Neff had to be guided on to the stage. Hers was unavoidably a heroic Mother Courage.

BRECHT'S DISCIPLES IN WEST GERMANY

Manker's breaking of the boycott heralded a Brecht boom in West Germany, particularly in the aftermath of student activism in 1968, a sad by-product of which was the persecution of Harry Buckwitz for his reputed Nazi past. The journal *Theater Heute*, which recorded German-language productions in Austria, Switzerland and the Federal Republic (not those in East Germany), lists thirty-nine professional stagings of Brecht's plays in the 1964/5 season (second to Shakespeare's sixty-seven). In 1967/8, 1972/3 and 1973/4, productions of Brecht's work outnumbered those of Shakespeare's, and the figures for the ten-year period from 1964/5 to 1973/4 make interesting reading:[5]

Shakespeare	616
Brecht	503
Molière	303
Schiller	287
Anouilh	210

Mother Courage participated in the boom from the start. Of particular interest is Peter Palitzsch's Cologne production in 1964. Palitzsch, after nearly a decade with the Berliner Ensemble, had left East Germany in 1960, taking with him the habit of documentation. His account of his approach to the production, published in *Theater Heute* (January 1965), is characteristically solemn. Nothing must be knowingly done on the stage that cannot be explained off it.

In an article of some 5,000 words, Palitzsch never mentions any of his actors by name (his Mother Courage was Ursula von Reibnitz). The characters of the play are reified, their function and the implications of their behaviour taking precedence over the details of performance. Palitzsch sees it as his directorial task to supervise the rendering of *Mother Courage* to the people of Cologne in 1964. Following Brecht's recommended approach even to his own plays, Palitzsch aimed to jettison accumulated preconceptions: 'In Brecht's theatre "one knows". But it begins with "not knowing". Naivety.'[6] Past solutions to staging problems are an impediment to the production *here* and *now*. The Berlin audience of 1949 needed no reminder that a play dealing with the Thirty Years War may resonate with the experience of 1939–45, but the same would not necessarily apply to Cologne in 1964. Palitzsch took an early decision about the Brechtian half-curtain with its 'light, fluttering waves of silk'. Since audiences had begun to get used to it, it must be changed, made strange again. The Cologne half-curtain would be made of the blood-red silk on which the Nazi emblem used to be stamped, and the scene-titles would be projected on to it in the bold black letters used in Nazi propaganda. The historical neutrality of the half-curtain was contradicted. It was made to overlap with a politically sinister flag; and the flag motif became scenically dominant as the performance progressed. As the geographical location of the action changed scene-by-scene, a historically appropriate flag was suspended against the upstage wall. These flags were allowed to accumulate, so that the single flag of the opening scene had, by the end, been joined by eleven others in a variety of splashing shapes and colours. The audience's last glimpse of Mother Courage was of an old woman dragging a dilapidated wagon towards a horizon overcast with the flags of vanished nation-states, many of them swallowed up by the new Germanies. Was there a visual reference to the vivid graffiti on the Berlin Wall in this obstructing wall of flags? Palitzsch makes no comment.

As in the film version, made with the Berliner Ensemble under the direction of Palitzsch and Manfred Wekwerth, the first scene opened on a stage that was empty save for a sparse avenue of saplings, and the final scene closed on a stage that was empty save for a scattering of blackened tree-stumps. At some risk of labouring Brecht's points, Palitzsch was determined to make everything clear. Mother Courage nursed her black silk shawl from start to finish. It was her passport to the bourgeoisie. The songs, delivered downstage with the lights dimmed behind the singer, lacked, in the view of some reviewers, the 'Brecht-bite', but Palitzsch's greater concern was with their meaning. He asked the actors to sing them with a minimum of theatricality and a maximum awareness of the quality of humanness that they shared with the audience. Dessau's score makes better room for the explosive consonants of German than for the variable vowels and muffled consonants of English, and Palitzsch properly insisted that the sound of the words was an essential accompaniment to the sound of the music. As always when working away from Berlin, he viewed his role as that of exemplifying Brecht's developed practice. He was less aware, perhaps, that he had assimilated some of the broadly psychological determinism of socialist realism. Mother Courage, he explains, is torn between economics and biology – trade and motherhood. She understands a lot, but has no insight.

The Cologne *Mother Courage* was visually attractive, set and costumes combining to create what Palitzsch called a 'beautiful disharmony', but it did not escape the kind of ponderousness of which the Berliner Ensemble directors stood accused in the years following Brecht's death. This accusation was levelled against Christoph Schroth in 1986, when he made the trip from East Berlin to Vienna to direct *Mother Courage* at the Burgtheater. 'This is the work of a model pupil of the Brecht-class and therefore quite school-masterly', wrote the *Theater Heute* reviewer,[7] and Klaus Völker, in a survey of Brecht productions on the German stage since 1945, refers to Schroth's as safe, 'dialectically and politically Brechtian, i.e. school-marmish'. There was, Völker continues:

> a little wit, a little finger-pointing, as if to say that war and peace exist in the world, but that war isn't really necessary. Brechtian lessons are taught in a gentle, friendly way . . . everything is as it should be, yet it doesn't work.[8]

Völker speaks for a view widely held in the German-speaking theatre; that programmatic productions of *Mother Courage* – those with the Model standing behind them – have little to say in countries that have no truck with Marx's hopes for humankind. Of course, if that is the mind-set of an audience, conversion is the only sure route to good reviews. Schroth made some concessions to the Austrian public by encouraging Elisabeth Orth to accentuate the jokiness, even warm-heartedness, of Mother Courage, but he failed to convince the majority of the reviewers. The critical tendency to equate the doctrinaire with the dull is as well established in Germany as it is in Britain.

Any director who tackles Brecht's plays is confronted by a dilemma. A respectful approach will lead to complaints of tedium. A less rigorous approach will turn many critics into sudden Brechtian purists. Wilfried Minks's jolly production of *Mother Courage* at the Deutsches Schauspielhaus in Hamburg, also in 1986, cast Eva Mattes as a charmingly cheeky flirt with a marked Bavarian accent. 'This is a Brecht love-in,' complains Völker, 'a cosy intimacy with Brecht, precisely where – especially with this anti-war theme – alienation, distance, shock are necessary to generate insights into the play.'[9] This 'heads I win, tails you lose' stance of critics towards productions of *Mother Courage* is common to virtually all first-world countries. A dutiful director, for whom the Model is a rehearsal bible, will be abused for dull purity by the same reviewer who castigates the impurity of a rival. As for the actress who presumes to play Mother Courage . . . she is walking into a mine-field of derogatory comparisons. When Harry Buckwitz directed Lotte Lenya in Recklinghausen in the summer of 1965, the *Düsseldorfer Nachrichten* began its review with the statement that 'Lotte Lenya does not correspond to the usual idea of Mother Courage', and the *Frankfurter Rundschau* was bluntly antagonistic:

> She's no actress. In normal prose, her voice is that of a singer who suddenly has to speak softly. Helene Weigel, Therese Giehse and Ursula von Reibnitz are far above her in their ability to convey the text.[10]

The vindictiveness of the press was disproportionate. It may have concealed an extra-theatrical resentment against an Austrian who had chosen to live in America and who now returned to Europe to claim a famous part in a play by a German who had turned his back on the Federal Republic. Lenya brought to the part an acquaintance with grief and with loneliness that she was, by 1965, wearing on her face. It was two years since her famous appearance as the sadistic Rosa Klebb in the James Bond film, *From Russia with Love*. She was not a no-hoper, nor, in this performance, did she deserve to be treated as one. Particularly in Germany, perhaps, the playing of Mother Courage may be read as an act of trespass.

BREAKING THE MOULD AT THE
SCHAUSPIELHAUS, BOCHUM, 1981

The Brecht boom in West Germany lasted until the late 1970s, to be succeeded by a period of what Werner Mittenzwei termed 'Brecht-fatigue'.[11] Renewed interest in the 1990s has been largely confined to the early plays, with which directors and actors have a greater sense of freedom. It seems, in the circumstances, unlikely that a production of *Mother Courage* as fresh as Alfred Kirchner's in Bochum in 1981 is imminent. Kirchner anchored the play in actuality whilst bombarding it with elements of the grotesque. In 1981 Iran was in the second year of its war with Iraq, and the United Nations were as powerless as ever to contain the aggression of member-states. Meanwhile, elections in the 'free' world were being won and lost on issues of tax until they had become, in Eric Hobsbawm's words, 'contests in fiscal perjury',[12] whilst the approach to global free trade (Mother Courage's dream) was making the rich nations richer and the poor nations legitimately exploitable. At the opening of the Bochum *Mother Courage*, a group of actors sat at the side of the stage watching a television monitor. After a while one of them stood up to spray the words 'For the Third World War' on a blackboard. 'Are we living on the edge of another war?' asked a talking head on the television screen. At chosen times throughout the performance, recorded excerpts from television programmes on current affairs dispensed information about the new technology of destruction, from neutron bombs to chemical warfare and beyond. Kirchner had tricks up his sleeve from the start. This was Brecht as the young Piscator might have liked to direct him. The cosy actors gathered round a piano, and the figure of Death, in a skeletal half-mask, emerged to perform a song-and-dance number: 'Without war there is no order; without order no war.' Only when Death had finished was the stage ready for the recruiters to begin their desultory debate: 'How can you have morality without a war, I ask you?'

The Bochum stage was sawdust-covered, not exactly a circus

ring but sufficiently like one to license the intermittent intervention of masked clowns and to provide a physical context for an Yvette who was self-consciously a showgirl. Death was the Master of Ceremonies, preparing the stage for and providing the titles to each scene. He was present throughout; plucking the dead Swiss Cheese to be his accomplice, lifting the injured infant in Scene 5 (Kattrin snatched it from him), crouching at a corner of the tent during the brief interlude of peace in Scene 8, signing receipts for the delivery of Mother Courage's dead children. Kirchner's theme was less consistently war than power. Who owns it? Politicians? Technocrats? And can it be wrested from them? It is a patriarchal world which this Kattrin in particular despairingly opposes, above all in the *coup de théâtre* of Scene 11. High on a gantry, Kattrin beat, not a single drum, but a whole set of drums which the inept soldiers had no way of silencing. The light changed to cold blue, and a fighter-plane – an actual Fiat G19 – descended from the flies to strafe her. Clinging to the side of the plane, Kattrin continued to beat it with a drumstick until it landed on the sawdust floor – the whole episode accompanied by the sound-track of John Lennon singing 'Imagine'. Once the plane had landed, quite coolly, two soldiers shot her.

Kirsten Dene played Mother Courage as a modern young woman, combative, energetic and sexy. Stefanie Carp, reviewing the production for *Theater Heute* (May 1981), found the first meeting of Mother Courage and the Cook so erotically played that she needed the words to remind her that the ostensible subject of the dialogue was a capon. In this uncommonly perceptive review, Carp compares the Bochum *Mother Courage* with a production of *Medea* in Düsseldorf: 'Two homeless women: Medea's suitcases, after her banishment by Kreon, are as constant a part of the set as Mother Courage's wagon on the Bochum stage.' How, she asks, can these women come to a sense of their own identity whilst their realities are projected and defined by men in power. Her conclusion, persuasively argued through reference to the productions, is that Medea triumphs in her own terms whilst Mother Courage's survival is the

Plate 7 Kattrin batters the fuselage of the plane that has just strafed her in Alfred Kirchner's 1981 production at the Bochum Schauspielhaus.

emblem of her continued subjugation. The evidence was there in Dene's playing of the final scene. Having sung the lullaby for her dead daughter, she carefully wiped her hands before stripping Kattrin (as in Schechner's New York production), folding her clothes and placing them on the empty wagon; a wagon dwarfed by the adjacent aeroplane. She then paid the peasants with Kattrin's earrings, kicked the wagon when she could not get it moving, and *pushed* it off, loudly singing, almost shouting, her song of war. 'She is not old,' writes Carp, 'not in rags and has acquired no knowledge.'

It is arguable that Dene's very modern Mother Courage, dressed in jeans for business and a smart dress for sex, has provided an alternative model to Weigel's. Wilful, zestful, an everyday woman with a gift for throw-away lines, she was much the same (looked much the same) at the end of the play as at its beginning. The horrifying truth was that her experience had not embittered her one iota. Dene embodied 'the great capitulation' on which the manipulators of the strings of power depend. In that sense, her performance was an acting out of the permanent war that George Orwell describes in *1984*:

> The war is waged by each ruling group against its own subjects, and the object of the war is not to make or prevent conquests of territory, but to keep the structure of society intact.

The Bochum *Mother Courage* was a particular interpretation of Brecht's dictum that 'war is the continuation of business by other means'.

THE BERLINER ENSEMBLE PRODUCTION, 1978

The theatre business was differently conducted in East Germany, where full employment was as much the rule for actors as for everybody else. It was not until 1949 that the subsidised theatres passed from Soviet control into the hands of the newly established government of the German Democratic Republic. Censorship remained strict, and was even strengthened after the Central Committee declared its opposition to formalism in 1951. The propaganda value of Brecht's name provided a measure of protection to the Berliner Ensemble, but some concession to Zhdanovite positivism was required even from this privileged company. As for the regional theatres, they were too nervous of their status to venture far into the Brechtian repertoire. *Senora Carrar's Rifles* was safe (and very popular), but *Mother Courage* was not. Only during the brief period of thaw following Brecht's death were his plays – *Mother Courage* among them – widely staged. There were twenty-one new productions of Brecht in East Germany in 1957 and twenty-nine in 1958. The Bitterfeld Conference of 1959 changed that. Playwrights were urged (instructed) there to adhere more closely to socialist ideology, to concentrate on establishing contact with workers, and to address more directly the condition of the Democratic Republic. Brecht's work was not banned, but it was incumbent on those who staged his plays judiciously to realign them according to Party policy. When performed in East Germany (and there were thirty-one productions from 1950 to 1977), *Mother Courage* was expected to provide more socialist uplift than the text readily offers.

Not only did the regional theatres of the Democratic Republic feel the looming presence of the Ministry of Culture behind them, they also had in front of them the threatening example of the Berliner Ensemble. *Mother Courage* remained in repertoire there throughout the 1950s. During that time the Ensemble, housed from 1954 in the quaintly ormolu Theater am Schiffbauerdamm, had acquired, largely to its own detriment, the reputation of a Brecht 'museum'. The most forceful of Brecht's young assistants, Manfred Wekwerth, was also the most doctrinaire. He approached the staging of plays with a scientific precision that Brecht would have admired, but with a humourlessness that not only limited his range but also brought him into unnecessary conflict with Helene Weigel. Wekwerth's rancorous departure in 1969 ushered in a decade of further controversy. When Weigel died in 1971, the nominal authority passed to Ruth Berghaus, who was temperamentally unsuited to the curatorship of a museum. Not only did she give priority to the production of new plays by young playwrights, but also gave offence to Brechtian conservatives in and around the Ensemble by offering theatrical revaluations of Brecht's canonical plays. Her dismissal (and the reappointment of Wekwerth in 1977) was a triumph of the old guard and a return to established routines in the Ensemble. Nothing was left to chance in Wekwerth's theatre, and there was always a danger that his meticulous work would have the chilliness of a blueprint. This was the defect of the 1978 production of *Mother Courage*, the first major undertaking of Wekwerth's regime, the first new production of the play by the Ensemble since 1949, and its thirty-third staging in East Germany.

The accredited director was Peter Kupke, and the Mother Courage, well established as actor and singer, was Gisela May. The production was documented with characteristic thoroughness and an unmistakable air of routine. The dominant impression, in reading the documentation, is of doggedness. Gisela May was specifically warned against cheerfulness. The cheerfulness of Weigel in the bombed city of Berlin in 1949 was, Kupke felt, appropriately frightening, but 'nowadays cheerfulness conceals everything. It must be clearly shown that war is the severest of all life's struggles.'[13] Why show the obvious, Brecht would surely have asked, unless you wish to show that the obvious is remarkable. A slightly bemused literalness pervades Kupke's commentary, as of a man who feels the need to unpack paradox and parse dialectics into an 'either . . . or . . . '. He is haunted by the Model, almost begging its pardon for seeking to incorporate the songs in the action. Kupke is trapped here between Brechtian *Verfremdung* and the dictates of socialist realism.

The production's intended emphasis was not on war, which Kupke saw merely as the play's starting-point, but on trade. Even so, it is by reference to the war that he distinguishes between the players:

> The seven leading characters display seven different attitudes to the war on the part of the little people. The attitudes contrast with one another. At the end of the play Courage is the wreck of her former self. The three children have been shot. Yvette is gross and sclerotic. The Chaplain has dwindled and can preach no more. Does the Cook ever reach Utrecht? The war is simply a given circumstance for the seven.[14]

Kupke's commentary – there are more than fifty pages of it in the official publication – reads like the work of a man who knows what ought to be said, but who was never quite sure what he ought to do. Wekwerth was watching. The merits of the production were incidental, not intrinsic. Its questionable proposal of Kattrin as Mother Courage's antagonist was not sustained in performance by the

Plate 8 The Drummer Boy speaks the titles for Scene 1 of the 1978
Berliner Ensemble production, directed by Peter Kupke.

homely Kattrin of Franziska Troegner. An innovation was the
opening of the play with a lone drummer-boy who, after a drum-
roll, spoke unemphatically the title-sentences of the first scene
before they were projected on to the half-curtain. Ekkehard Schall
played the Cook in the belief that he is 'from first to last a swine'.[15] It
was a part he found difficult to make his own after so long playing
Eilif alongside Ernst Busch's Cook.

Most of the Berlin reviewers found the production worthy but
unexciting. Gisela May was compared unfavourably with Helene
Weigel. Wekwerth had criticised in rehearsal her tendency to play
Mother Courage as a female Schweyk. This is something about
which Brecht himself was ambivalent. On the one hand, having
completed the writing of *Puntila*, he noted: 'the tone is not original,
it is hasek's way of speaking in schweyk, as already used by me in

COURAGE',[16] and on the other, 'SCHWEYK largely finished. a counter-play to MOTHER COURAGE'.[17] Wekwerth had no such mixed feelings. Conscious of the danger that Schweykian slyness (rather than Weigel's anger) was guiding May's delivery of the lines, he advised her to seek out the dryness of the language.[18] The point of her performance that received the greatest critical acclaim came in the final scene. It may have owed its provenance to Buckwitz and Lotte Lenya in Recklinghausen. Having sung her lullaby over the dead Kattrin, May gestured to the peasants to give her a moment alone with the body. Then, crawling under the tarpaulin that covered it, she laid her face against Kattrin's for a held beat. Having paid the peasants, she deliberately summoned up the memory of her lost sons as she lifted in turn the rein of the wagon that had been Eilif's and the rein that had been Swiss Cheese's. If this was sentimentality, it was probably indistinguishable from socialist realism.

THE THÉÂTRE NATIONAL POPULAIRE IN SURESNES, 1951

The earliest performance of a non-German *Mother Courage* opened in 1946 in Turku (Finland), and before 1970 the play had been produced in Belgium, Iceland, France, Sweden, Poland, Israel, Mexico, Holland, the Soviet Union, New Zealand, Denmark, Bulgaria, Cuba, Norway, Romania, Brazil, Ireland, Hungary, Yugoslavia, Canada, Chile and Italy. Scarcely one of the these productions had any impact outside its own immediate environment and theatrical circle. The same is true of most German productions, of course. The production at the Kassel Staatstheater in 1960 by even so notable a director as Erwin Piscator has sunk without trace. John Willett, himself a notable Brechtian, does not consider it worth a mention in his account of Piscator's life in the theatre.[19] *Mother Courage* would seem to be a play through which directors rarely make their

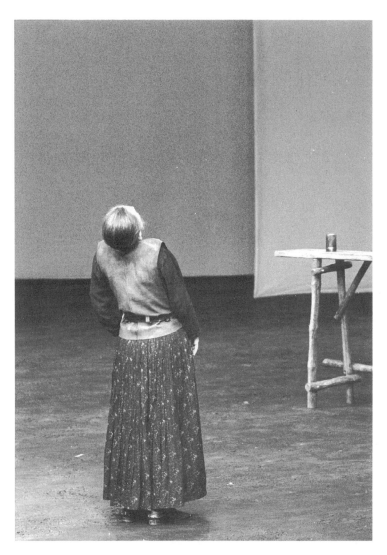

Plate 9 Conscious of Helene Weigel's famous posture for the silent scream in Scene 3, Gisela May chose to hide her face from the audience of the 1978 Berliner Ensemble production.

reputation and actresses regularly risk theirs. In this respect, Jean Vilar's production for the Théâtre National Populaire in 1951 is exceptional, less in itself than for what it represented.

Like Brecht in Berlin in 1949, Vilar chose *Mother Courage* to initiate an enterprise of national importance. The quest for a people's theatre in France had already a long and turbulent history. France is a country peculiarly hospitable to discourses of culture, and one in which the artistic dominance of the *élite* (the English language has had to borrow the word from the French) has been constantly challenged. A Théâtre National Populaire had been established in 1920 under the management of Firmin Gémier, whose vision was of a touring theatre dedicated to the carriage of festive performance around the country. For many of his artistically influential compatriots, Gémier, who had created the role of Père Ubu in Jarry's *Ubu Roi* (1896), was a vulgarian. Inadequately funded, the venture faltered, and the attempts of the Popular Front government to revive it after the election of 1936 were misguided. Simply by rebuilding the vast complex of the Palais de Chaillot and providing it with an auditorium that could accommodate 2,800, the Popular Front hoped to establish a theatre for the people in the heart of Paris's fashionable sixteenth *arrondissement*. At the end of World War II the Théâtre National Populaire was moribund and the theatrical dominance of Paris almost absolute. Against the fifty-two theatres in the capital, there were only fifty-one in the rest of France, nearly all of them empty shells intermittently filled by professional touring companies or local amateurs. But the experience of wartime occupation and of the Resistance movement had fostered in France new hopes for social unity. The communal art of theatre was uniquely placed to express these hopes, and Jean Vilar became their embodiment.

Through his mentor Charles Dullin, Vilar was the inheritor of two French traditions, one deriving from Gémier and the other from Jacques Copeau, with both of whom Dullin had worked. Copeau's bare stage, on which the actors could display their craft in its purity, was designed to make plays more accessible to audiences, above all by peeling away the mystifications of theatrical trickery. Vilar the ascetic acknowledged the influence of Copeau's *tréteau nu*. But he was an admirer also of Gémier's festive theatre, which he carried further than Gémier ever could in the summer seasons at Avignon. Vilar initiated these seasons in 1947 and retained his involvement in them until his death in 1971. The Avignon performances were staged without décor, and played in the open air on a platform of variable dimensions set against a courtyard wall of the Papal Palace. Vilar encouraged his actors to drink, eat and mingle with the audience before and after performances. Understandably, Jean Caune places Vilar at the point of intersection between Gémier, the initiator of a popular theatre in France, and Copeau, its prophet.[20] It was on the strength of his work in Avignon that Vilar was appointed director of the Théâtre National Populaire in 1951.

The task was a formidable one. The TNP was still formally confined to the vast Palais de Chaillot, and its funding was insufficient to protect it from commercial pressures. But Vilar, as well as being an adroit entrepreneur, was popular with his fellow-professionals. He brought to the job a broad belief in cultural democracy which may appear naive in the retrospect of *fin de siècle* scepticism, but which can reasonably claim to have made a major contribution to the post-war transformation of theatrical culture in France. 'We will not be tempted to choose easy works in order to attract our audience', he promised,[21] although he knew well that his famous wish to 'assemble and unite' called for immediate attention to assembly. It was as much a symbolic as a practical gesture to hold the inaugural performances of the new TNP away from its Parisian headquarters. The first poster is, in its own right, a fascinating theatrical document. Beginning on 17 November 1951 at the Théâtre de Suresnes, it announces, there will be fifteen performances of Corneille's *Le Cid* and Brecht's *Mother Courage* (no mention of the children). There is then a list of the actors in the company, in alphabetical order so that Vilar's is the penultimate of twenty-one names, and a statement of seat-prices (from 100 to 250 francs). The bottom third of the poster, boxed in, advertises three 'Week-ends Artistiques', presented by Jean Vilar and constituting 'Le petit festival de Suresnes', the weekends to include meals, a dance, a concert, performances of both the plays in the repertoire, and, exceptionally on 17 November, Maurice Chevalier (Vilar had marketable contacts). Bus number 144 leaves from the Pont de Neuilly, and the return bus journey is guaranteed.

Suresnes was one of the 'red-belt' suburbs of Paris, predominantly working-class and controlled by communist authorities. Except for a brief period in his youth, Vilar had no formal links with the Communist Party, and, although his leanings were always to the left, he valued social unification above the divisiveness of politics in his strategy for the TNP:

> To this concern, which is to assemble in our troubled times men and women of all religious and political beliefs, I will add the daily attempts to do well and to act in the interests of an audience which has usually been deprived of such joys. For this audience, wherever we are, we will present the stark shape of the stage, with no ornaments, no sleight of hand, no scenery.[22]

Neither the ideology nor the aesthetic is well suited to a production of *Mother Courage*, a play which, despite the evident simplicity of its narrative, makes technical demands that are inseparable from its meaning. Vilar's natural preference was for plays of heroism and pathos. *Le Cid*, companion-piece to *Mother Courage* in the opening programme, was carried over from the Avignon Festival, where Gérard Philipe's heroic/pathetic Rodrigue had been universally applauded. Vilar chose to match the charismatic Philipe, whom Kenneth Tynan thought 'the best jeune premier in the world, a limpid, lyrical young animal',[23] with the highly emotional Germaine Montéro as Mother Courage. 'What struck me about the play was its profound optimism,' wrote Vilar, 'the confidence which Brecht places in the human being.'[24] The observation is ambiguous. Brecht places his confidence in the changeability of the human beings in the audience. Vilar evidently placed his in Mother Courage. For Bernard Dort, the first Brecht scholar among French critics, the result was that 'pathos triumphed over statement; we were shown not an action, but a passion'.[25] Critical reception in France was lukewarm when it was not downright hostile, but Vilar refused to be deterred. *Mother Courage* remained in the TNP repertoire until 1960, by which time it had been performed to more than 140,000 people. Among non-French plays, only Kleist's *Prince of Hombourg*, starring Gérard Philipe, was given more performances under Vilar's regime.

When Kenneth Tynan, on one of his periodic trips in search of brickbats to hurl at the London stage, saw Vilar's production of *Mother Courage*, his response was exaggeratedly positive. The play had by then transferred to the Palais de Chaillot:

> About the TNP's production of Brecht's *Mère Courage* I have no reservations at all: a glorious performance of a contemporary classic which has been acclaimed everywhere in Europe save in London . . . Does Germaine Montéro, as the sleazy, irresistible heroine, nag where she should dominate? Yes – but the play carries her. Never before have I seen a thousand people rise cheering and weeping in their seats.[26]

The exaggeration is palpable, and Brecht would not have been gratified by the weeping of even one. Vilar's production was vivacious where Brecht's was deliberate. The tempo was altogether faster, and Montéro, under encouragement from her director, made Mother Courage's durability a triumph and her occasional drunkenness a sympathetic compensation. Writing in 1955, Tynan had not yet seen the Berliner Ensemble's production. Several Parisians had, when it won first prize at the International Theatre Festival in 1954. The American director Alan Schneider was there, and remembered three years later:

> . . . on the apron of the Sarah Bernhardt, Brecht's tumultuous *Mother Courage* played on a half-bare turntable – in a breath-taking

production which blended the finest Actors' Studio realism with the most eloquent of Japanese theatre 'style'.[27]

David Bradby goes so far as to call the Paris staging of the Berlin *Mother Courage* the turning-point in the French *théâtre populaire* movement.[28] Its effect in France was even greater and more immediate than its effect in England two years later. Between 1954 and the *évènements* of 1968, Brecht's was the major influence in the French theatre, despite the brilliance of Beckett and the anti-political diatribes of Ionesco. The journal *Théâtre Populaire*, founded to further Vilar's work and including both Barthes and Dort among its contributing editors, contained the first reasoned critique of Brecht's theory and practice; and in 1955 the publishing house of L'Arche brought out the first in its twelve-volume translation of Brecht's work. Away from Paris, the brilliant young director Roger Planchon was fired by the notion of 'scenic writing', the semiotic system by which Brecht aimed to extend the playwright's text into performance. Productions of Brecht's plays spread across France and were greeted with the kind of enthusiasm that made British reservations appear anti-intellectual. At Toulouse in 1959 Jacques Mauclair directed *Mother Courage* with one eye on the Model Book. A trade union group performed the play in Bressieux in 1965. There were major productions after 1968, too; by Antoine Vitez's company at Ivry in 1973, and by the Théâtre des Amandiers in Nanterre in 1975. But Brecht had by then ceased to be, in any marketable sense, a popular playwright. Vilar's brave bid to absorb him into the cultural self-discovery of the unified French nation had been overbid by circumstance. When the TNP was passed over to Planchon in Lyons in 1972, Vilar's vision of an assembled and united people was already viewed as a chimera. Planchon's perception is of a radically divided France, in which there is a danger of cultural domination by the few: 'our job is to keep the wound open'.[29]

As the twentieth century approaches its end, *Mother Courage* is sliding backwards into cultural history. I received a postcard some years ago, one of those satirical photo-montage images in which the then Mrs Thatcher had taken Helene Weigel's place between the shafts of Mother Courage's wagon. It was the play's final tableau, and the card asked where Mrs Thatcher was dragging the wagon from, and where to. A production which cast Lady Thatcher as Mother Courage would provide a nice exercise in dialectics. As things are, the play carries with it into performance a sense of having, temporarily at least, lost its battle to unworthy victors. For Bernard Dort, writing from a French perspective:

> It is not a question of returning to an unqualified adoption of Brecht, nor of totally rejecting him with the exception of a few texts. Rather, one should start by acknowledging his lack of relevance (which does not exclude the possibility that one might from time to time underline his contemporaneity). Brecht's work has become historical. To present him is to relativize him or to 'distance' him. It is to take account of the distance that separates us from him. It is to recognize how tangential he is to the history of the last thirty years.

All too aware of the danger of ascribing to Brecht the monumental status of a classical playwright, Dort holds his ground:

> If we have to relativize him it is because in this way we will be able to preserve him. In this way we will be true to his objectives and to his dreams: the vision of a theatre and of a world united in its contradictions, which is constantly changing and transforming itself.[30]

This is a modest recovery, but a realistic one. Trying to explain her reasons for acting, Fiona Shaw has suggested that 'the desire to perform is the desire to make sense of the world by performing in it'.[31] *Mother Courage* can still, surely, strengthen that desire in actor and audience.

CHAPTER SIX

THE AFTERLIFE OF
MOTHER COURAGE

In December 1955, a few months after the Theatre Workshop production in Barnstaple, R. D. Smith directed *Mother Courage* for the
BBC Third Programme – a typically bold stroke from a noted
ground-breaker. I no longer remember how much I heard before
switching it off. I knew nothing about Brecht at the time, but I kept
a teenage notebook. 'Strange German play,' it reads. 'Boring'. I take
some comfort from the observations of John Drakakis:

> No adequate correlative has been found in radio for the deliberate
> aberrations of theatrical form upon which a Brecht play depends for
> its effects. Even the flexibility of the medium – which can take in tight
> or episodic structures – cannot cope, since the constant pressure to
> which it is subjected is that of making the unfamiliar familiar and
> encouraging the listener's collusion to this end. The result is that the
> iconoclastic vitality of Brecht's plays, with their constant focus upon
> form itself, is reduced on radio to series of familiar variety acts, held
> together by an even more familiar radio figure, the narrator.[1]

It is difficult to imagine a better radio production than Jeremy
Mortimer's on BBC Radio Three in May 1990. The Dessau score
was used in full, and a narrator used only to read the scene-titles.
Sheila Hancock's vocal and tonal range was a huge asset, and John
Willett's adaptation of his translation for radio was astute. Mortimer
maintained a tight control of the narrative. But, almost inevitably
where stage groupings are irrelevant, the socio-political force of the
play was rendered insufficient. It became an intensely personal
domestic drama. This was partly the outcome of the producer's
attempt to grapple with the problem of Kattrin (what to do with a

mute in a radio play). This was a Kattrin who chuckled, grunted, laughed, almost gargled; and great stress was laid on the relationship between mother and daughter. This was Hancock at the warmest end of her vocal register, and the effect was to make the play domestic and familial at its centre. Even so well considered a production tended to confirm the impossibility of doing justice to *Mother Courage* outside the theatre. What Drakakis says of Brecht on radio applies *mutatis mutandis* to Brecht on film or television. *Mother Courage* has, of itself, no interesting history outside the theatre. There is a simple reason for that. The play is artfully written for the stage, whose physical limitations are the conditions that release its energy. It is presented to a particular audience in a particular place at a particular time, and neither its narrative nor its characters have a life independent of the theatre. This is not to deny Brecht's influence on the European cinema, which was particularly strong during the 1970s. Jean-Luc Godard was openly indebted to Brechtian techniques in his quest for a politically effective aesthetic. Jean Marie Straub looked to Brecht for both subject-matter and acting style. Rainer Werner Fassbinder appropriated the principle of separated epic scenes. A carefully selective argument could draw in film-makers as various as Woody Allen and Peter Greenaway. But there is a danger of making too much of comparatively little. Thomas Elsaesser's summary is judicious:

> Not only did Brecht come to stand for a very complex set of assumptions and practices among film-makers and for film theory of the 1970s; his teachings played a crucial role in the much wider cultural shift which marked the avant-garde's final break with high modernism.[2]

It was Brecht's method of separating out the elements of a narrative – laying them open for scrutiny – that first tempted film-makers. The result, quite often, has been a self-conscious display of the medium that has nothing discernibly to do with *Mother Courage*. It is probably not with this play that those who argue for Brecht's influence on film theory are concerned.

The surviving film of *Mother Courage* exhibits little more than the documentary capacity of the medium. It was made in 1960–61 as a joint venture by the Berliner Ensemble and the East German state company DEFA, employed the full cast of the current stage version just before it was removed from the repertoire, and was directed by Manfred Wekwerth and Peter Palitzsch, whose directorial credentials were theatrical rather than cinematic. It is a visual record of a memorable production, although cuts were made to fit it more closely to conventions of screen-time. Unframed by stage-walls, the settings have a bleak unreality. Only the performances present themselves in their solidity. The dominant impression is of unhurried conversations briefly interrupted by flurries of activity. Dessau's charmless music is matched by singing that offers no gesture towards charm. In extreme contrast to the Hollywood musical (1961 was the year of *West Side Story*), the songs are simply presented, not *sold*, to the camera. Weigel does nothing superfluous. Her mode is to let time pass until the next thing must be done. Ekkehard Schall's Eilif-dance in Scene 2 (the 'scenes' are divided by voice-over readings of the titles) is a virtuoso combination of economy and agility: the control is balletic. Busch's Cook is phlegmatic: pausing briefly near a signpost in an empty landscape, he makes his final exit with scarcely a glance at the retreating wagon. Hurwicz's Kattrin ranges from the grotesquely comic to the overwhelmingly pathetic: her facial expressions, seen in close-up at her death, are as graphic as those in a silent-film melodrama. It is the only sensationalised sequence. Only once is there a serious attempt to exploit the dexterity of the camera. This is in Scene 10, when the camera becomes the eyes of the invisible singer, looking from inside the house through the frost-coated window at Kattrin and Mother Courage, halted in the snow. The whole amounts to a film of the play – not a filmic interpretation. It records and repeats the rhythms of the stage performance; the slow sweep of the narrative, the concentration on a group of people who evince no awareness that they are contributing to anything that might be called a narrative. At its best, the texture resembles that of a film by Ingmar Bergman, but there is nothing Brechtian about Bergman's metaphysical probings.

If *Mother Courage* has significance only in the theatre, its impact there has been, if ultimately immeasurable, enduring. Brecht's production with the Berliner Ensemble challenged, and to some extent changed, attitudes to the directing (and therefore acting) of plays in the European theatre. The inclusion of Dessau's score and his treatment of the songs carried the idea of a 'music theatre' into new thematic territory. For certain playwrights, the historicising of contemporary issues exemplified by *Mother Courage* opened both past and present to critical scrutiny, the outcome of which was a new kind of 'history' play. These three areas of effect – on directing, on music theatre and on dramaturgy – will be separately treated in this final chapter. My aim is less to close an argument than to indicate the terms in which an argument might be conducted and some of the items that might be used to illustrate it.

'MOTHER COURAGE' AND THE DIRECTOR: PETER BROOK AND OTHERS

It was through working on *Mother Courage* in East Berlin that Brecht established his own directorial practices, and it was the touring of the production that provoked directors in many countries to reassess their priorities. It is notoriously difficult to define influence, and the pursuit of definition culminates all too often in oversimplification or platitude. The circumstances in which Brecht and the Berliner Ensemble created *Mother Courage* cannot be reproduced, but the outcome was visible through the 1950s, and is still visible in the unsatisfactory film version. What most impressed theatrical professionals was a previously unimagined realism that owed nothing to the illusion of reality. Everything on stage was there to be used by the actors. There was no attempt to provide an authenticating scenic environment – no backdrops or cycloramas, no battlefield images, no skyscapes. On an undisguised stage, human interactions of a defiantly unstagey kind occurred as if under no pressure from theatrical time. For a director, time in the theatre is generally associated with the pacing of successive episodes: speed in picking up cues, split-second precision of entrances, the breakneck as a preferable alternative to the ponderous. If these were concerns for the Berliner Ensemble, they were not evidently so. The production responded to its own imperatives, not to the pre-existent imperatives of theatrical convention. It stood its own ground.

One of the important consequences of the *Mother Courage* tours was a heightened awareness of the dynamic relationship between the direction of a play and its setting. The later development of conflicting performance theories has one of its sources in this awareness. *Mother Courage* seemed to its early onlookers to transform whatever theatre it occupied; they might be as various as the Theater am Schiffbauerdamm in Berlin, the Sarah Bernhardt in Paris and the Palace in London. The pictorial stage inherited from the nineteenth century was stripped and humbled, the playing space cleared for occupation by the actors. The possibility that the performance might dictate terms to the building that housed it was a liberating one. It would be developed in many different ways: by Jerzy Grotowski in Poland, Ariane Mnouchkine in France, Peter Stein in West Germany, Schechner in the USA. That is to say that the production of *Mother Courage* carried with it, wherever it went, the seeds of an environmental theatre. It is not, however, to such performances that the label 'Brechtian' has most commonly been applied. Since I intend to propose a dialectical relationship between Brecht's work on *Mother Courage* and Peter Brook's on *US*, I should clear some ground.

After the Berliner Ensemble's visit to London in 1956, British critics began to apply Brecht's name to almost any production of a 'serious' play on a bare stage. The attention of theatregoers was drawn, in particular, to a new trend in the staging of Shakespeare's history plays. When the Royal Shakespeare Company, in 1963, brought together the three parts of *Henry VI* and *Richard III* under the generic title of *The Wars of the Roses*, the adjectives 'epic' and 'Brechtian' were lavishly applied. There was some justification for this. Peter Hall and John Barton were certainly in pursuit of a sparser, narrative style of playing that owed something to the Berlin *Mother Courage* and very little to the strutting heroism of the Bensonian tradition. And John Bury's design focused on scenic pieces rather than on the scenic environment of pictorial convention. These scenic pieces were not stage mock-ups. They were made of genuine steel. The actors moved and grouped around and among authentic material. But Hall and Barton are not Brechtian directors. When Barton rewrote or plumped out the Shakespearean text (and he did quite a lot of that at Stratford during the 1960s and early 1970s), it was not to serve the purposes of socio-political intervention but to supply a corrective dramaturgy. Brecht had a different way with *Coriolanus*. It is not particularly useful to label as Brechtian a production that employs a spatter of words from Brecht's theatrical vocabulary. It is not the design on stage that distinguishes a Brechtian production, but the design on the audience. The keyword here is *Gestus*.

Gestus has no strict equivalent in English, and attempts to provide it with one have tended to complicate our understanding. A problem is that Brecht's use of the word calls simultaneously on the separate crafts of playwright, actor and director. It refers to the attitude of the invented character, the demonstrative behaviour of the performer of the invented character, and the physical relationship between all the invented characters on stage at any given time. In broad terms, the first of these is determined by the playwright, the second by the actor, and the third by the director. But Brecht, for whom the mingling of the three crafts became habitual through the rehearsal of *Mother Courage*, used *Gestus* sometimes to apply to any one of its facets, or even, as Kim Kowalke has affirmed, to music and musicians:

> Within the dramaturgy of a music-theatre which strove to illuminate
> social relationships between characters rather than internal psycho-
> logical states, Weill and Brecht both conceived *Gestus* as a means of
> making manifest on stage the behaviour and attitudes of human
> beings towards one another.[3]

This is the concept of social *Gestus* whose clarity and intelligence
Barthes celebrated,[4] and through which he located the autonomous
language of setting and action ('scenic writing') in Brecht's production of *Mother Courage*. It is a concept more readily understood by
directors than it has been by scholars. It is the most basic task of a
director, when blocking a play, to establish effective groupings of
characters on the stage. It was Brecht's innovation to make such
groupings indicators of meaning, socio-political statements whose
detail would be painstakingly established in rehearsal. The final
decisions were taken in collaboration with the actors, whose opinions were respected. The significance of this was well understood by
Peter Brook:

> What Brecht introduced was the idea of the intelligent actor, capable
> of judging the value of his contribution. There were and still are many
> actors who pride themselves on knowing nothing about politics and
> who treat the theatre as an ivory tower. For Brecht such as an actor is
> not worthy of his place in adult company: an actor in a community
> that supports a theatre must be as much involved in the outside
> world as in his own craft.[5]

The Empty Space, from which this quotation is taken, was published
in 1968, but it was based on lectures delivered a year earlier, when
the shock-waves of Brook's production of *US* were still crashing.
Much coloured by a personality very different from Brecht's, *US*
offers complex and contradictory evidence of directorial debt to
Brecht in general and to *Mother Courage* in particular.

Brook had seen the Berliner Ensemble production as early as
1950, when he was in Berlin to negotiate the rights to stage the play
with the Group Theatre in London. Nearly forty years later he

recalled that 'in [Brecht's] production of *Mother Courage* . . . I found
that however much he tried to break any belief in the reality of what
happened on the stage, the more he did, the more I entered whole-
heartedly into the illusion'.[6] Brook concludes the statement with an
exclamation mark. I am not sure why, unless it is an attempt to
revive excitement through punctuation. Brook should, after all,
know that his was not an uncommon experience. He is guilty of
entering a debate at the wrong point. Brecht's quarrel was not with
emotional engagement, certainly not with reality, but with empathy.
The *Verfremdungseffekte* implicitly allow for emotional engagement
on the part of the audience. They are interruptions designed to
return the spectators to a sense of themselves in the here and now. If
there were no fictional flow, there would be nothing to interrupt. In
his retrospect, Brook recalls the flow and denies the effect of the
interruptions: but who, remembering a Cup Final years later, retains
the memory of that moment when a professional foul brought into
focus a personal morality? More than anything else, it was Brook's
inclination to polarise intellect and emotion that spoiled *US*. In this
respect, both through rehearsal and in performance, it stands in
exemplary tension with *Mother Courage*.

US was an extraordinary experiment, conducted in private but
intended always for public demonstration under the banner of the
Royal Shakespeare Company. The opening was already scheduled
for October when the actors were called for their first meeting on
the most significant day in the American calendar – 4 July 1966.
Albert Hunt's moody description of the occasion is part of the long
Introduction to the published text:

> Brook began by re-stating his belief in a theatre that could speak
> directly about contemporary issues. The theatre ought to have a voice
> that could be listened to seriously. The trouble was that people found
> it only too easy to dismiss what they had seen as just another theatrical
> success . . . We needed to make a statement that a Wilson or a
> Johnson would not be able to shrug off in this way. At the same time,
> we must be aware from the start that we were not trying to make a

> documentary about Vietnam. We were going to examine our own
> attitudes, to ask ourselves as totally as possible how the Vietnam
> War affected *us*.[7]

The eventual confusion of *US*, embodied in its enigmatic title – US
is the people of Britain, US is America, US is this particular group of
co-workers – is already latent in the final sentence of that quotation.
It was never the effect of war on the individual selves of Weigel,
Hurwicz, Busch and Schall that Brecht wished to explore through
the rehearsals of *Mother Courage*; it was their attitude towards war as
business. But Brecht would certainly have understood the sources of
Brook's initial questioning, and Brook was conscious of Brecht
behind him:

> Brecht is the key figure of our time, and all theatre work today at some
> point starts or returns to his statements and achievement . . . It was
> out of respect for the audience that Brecht introduced the idea of
> alienation, for alienation is a call to halt: alienation is cutting, inter-
> rupting, holding something up to the light, making us look again.
> Alienation is above all an appeal to the spectator to work for himself,
> so to become more and more responsible for accepting what he sees
> only if it is convincing him in an adult way. Brecht rejects the roman-
> tic notion that in the theatre we all become children again.[8]

Writing that in the immediate aftermath of *US*, Brook is reflecting
on the interaction between Brecht's theatrical processes and his own.
His rejection of a remote theatre entombed in 'culture' had Brecht as
a historical precedent. But had *Mother Courage* gone far enough?
Was Brecht too reasonable? Like Brecht, although in the particular
context of the Vietnam War, Brook wished to expose and make
strange the human tendency to avoid facing up to the truth.
'Whatever the cost,' he noted about his work on *US*, 'a man mar-
shalls everything at his disposal to skid away from the simple
recognition of how things are.'[9] *Mother Courage*, it now seemed to
him, had permitted him to skid away with the rest of humankind.
How was he to prevent audiences from doing the same with *US*?
This was the era of the Happening – the spectacular interruption of

normality that may buttonhole random spectators and force them to take notice. Always eclectic, Brook explored Happenings:

> The alienation effect and the happening effect are similar and opposite: the happening shock is there to smash through all the barriers set up by our reason, alienation is to shock us into bringing the best of our reason into play.[10]

To challenge the audience's orderly avoidance of the truth, *US* would, at key moments, exploit the disorderliness of the Happening. In this way, Brook believed, it might carry *Mother Courage* towards a theatre of confrontation.

The first need was to create an ensemble, in pursuit of which Brook called on some of the actors with whom he had worked on Peter Weiss's *Marat/Sade* two years earlier. As he describes it himself, 'Twenty-five actors in a close relationship with an authors' team set out to do an investigation of the Vietnamese situation, and this took a number of months.'[11] In a radical departure from Brechtian practice they began without a text. The intention was to construct a text out of discoveries made by the actors, and to employ a writer to shape a final version. Charles Wood, whose *Cockade* (1963) had demonstrated a vivid response to the language of militarism, was the intended dramaturg, but he was unable to attend rehearsals and withdrew a few weeks into the project. Act 1 was scripted by an authorial team on the basis of research and improvisation by the ensemble. In broad terms, its mode is that of the theatrical documentary, providing initially some background information on Vietnamese history and culture and then setting particular incidents into the framework of the Vietnam War. In performance, it was a technically ambitious and often spectacular collage in which songs, composed by the (token?) American Richard Peaslee, were a major feature. The actors, casually dressed in clothes which were probably their own, moved around the Aldwych stage under the huge inflated dummy of a soldier, which crashed to and cumbersomely settled on the floor towards the Act's end. In a strangely confused review for the *Listener*, Bryan Magee called *US* 'a firework display of theatrical skill', whilst complaining that the whole production 'hypocritically disregards its own point that to be anti-American is as racialist, vile and irrational as to be anti-semitic; what it presents are not the facts of the situation but the fictions of communist propaganda'. This leads Magee to the mysterious conclusion that 'the first and longer part of the evening is little better than superior Brecht'.[12] A better-informed reviewer might have complained that *US* was Brechtian only in its designs on the audience and its reliance on intelligent actors. Act 2, largely the product of Denis Cannan's shaping, was intensely personal. Cannan thought of Act 1 as 'centering on man and his predicament while Act 2 should focus on man and his nature'.[13] The utterness of the contrast took the audience by surprise. The still focus of Act 2 was the single actor, Mark Jones, whose task it was to sustain a determination to burn himself to death in protest against the war in the face of passionate counter-persuasion, above all from Glenda Jackson. The burning itself was represented, at the end of the piece, by the burning of a butterfly, after which the actors remained on stage, silent and unmoving, until all the audience had left. What the whole event illustrates is the extent to which a particular director, in pursuit of broadly Brechtian ends and conscious of that, may use distinctly un-Brechtian means.

The crucial determinant was Brook's view that the Berliner Ensemble's *Mother Courage* failed in its purpose. *US* replaced the dialectical with the direct. It was all terribly in earnest. At the end, confronted by those silent actors, I felt guilty, angry and embarrassed. The guilt came easily. Of course I should have known more, done more about the Vietnam War. The anger was an immediate response to the silence of the actors; they were staring at us in what might well have been a holier-than-thou manner. Brook's explanation of this conclusion contradicts my experience of it:

> When the actors sit in silence at the end of *US*, they are reopening the question, each night, for all of us, of where we stand at this moment here and now in relation to what is going on in ourselves and the world around us. The very end of *US* is certainly not, as some have

taken it to be, an accusation or reproach to the audience from the actors. The actors are truly concerned with themselves; they are using and confronting what is most scary in themselves.[14]

How was Brook to know that? And how were we? Nothing so incalculable was admitted by Brecht. Nor do I believe that the decision to end *US* in this way was as innocent as Brook implies. The actors had been through a gruelling rehearsal process, some of it almost cruelly exposing. They might have felt that they had earned the right to embarrass the audience. In fact, though, I was embarrassed *for* as well as *by* the actors. What Irving Wardle called the 'vicarious psychodrama'[15] of Act 2 made them vulnerable. Brook's mode of directing his actors was not unlike Moreno's mode of directing his patients – probing, prompting and, in intention, therapeutic. One rehearsal session may stand as an example. In the room were Brook, five members of the authorial team and the single actor, Mark Jones. It was Jones's task to defend the decision to burn himself against the prepared arguments successively of Denis Cannan, Adrian Mitchell and Albert Hunt. Finally came Brook:

> Brook sat down on the floor with Mark. Very close to him. 'Look me in the eye. What is cruelty? Unlimited exercise of power over others. Do you have power over other people? Do you have power over yourself? Aren't you being cruel to your own flesh by setting it on fire? Aren't you alive? What is you? There is something called life and it's there in you. Have you the right to destroy it? What you want to do to yourself is what the world is doing to itself. You want life for the world, why don't you allow yourself to live? If you stop now, one less act of cruelty has taken place. It takes more courage to face the situation than to burn yourself. It takes the same kind of courage for the super-powers involved in this war to back down from their prepared positions.'

Michael Kustow, whose commentary this is, adds an evaluative point:

> Mark put his head in his hands. There was silence for five minutes. The exercise had lasted nearly two hours. We all sat still. I was very

aware of the different kind of contact Brook had made with the actor compared with the others. Brook's questioning had been much more physical, much closer to a confessional.[16]

It would be difficult to imagine a less Brechtian rehearsal. No irony, no humour, no permitted distance between the actor and his 'text'. What had begun as a Brecht-inspired quest for a theatrical voice on contemporary issues that 'could be listened to seriously' culminated, after the ensemble had been subjected to intense pressure, in an emotional barrage of the audience. B. A. Young spoke for many reviewers in finding *US* 'directed exclusively at the emotions',[17] and Bryan Magee had completed a volte-face by the end of the evening:

> My emotional complacency has not been so shattered, my defences so pierced and prised open and the naked, elementary feeling exposed, since I saw *King Lear* in the same theatre done by the same company under the same director, four years ago. In the last quarter of its second part *US* transcends its own faults so far that they come to seem unimportant, as I now firmly believe they are.[18]

The turning-point had come in the fourth week of rehearsal, when Jerzy Grotowski began a ten-day workshop with the actors.

It is fairly clear that Grotowski annihilated whatever was Brechtian in the project. Michael Kustow found the workshop difficult to describe 'because it took place on such a private naked level':

> . . . it was in every sense a workshop, a consulting-room, a confessional, a temple, a refuge, a place of reflection conducted not only with the mind, but with every fibre and muscle of the body.[19]

Grotowski treated actors as a priesthood, thus bolstering the hieratic in Brook's own temperament. By the end of this workshop a political mission had become a sacred one. Whatever was left of Brecht was merely vestigial. But *US* remains of significance in a discussion of *Mother Courage* because it raised with peculiar urgency and force questions about the ability of the theatre to make itself heard in the world. That the project took itself extremely seriously is clear from the tortured pages of the published text and commentary: itself a neurotic version of a Brechtian Model Book. For Irving Wardle, *US* was 'something new in the British theatre';[20] for Charles Marowitz, it was 'nothing more than Living Newspaper technique brought up to date';[21] for the Bishop of Woolwich, it was liturgy, 'nothing separating stage from stalls, sanctuary from congregation'.[22] It was nearly eighteen years since the Berlin première of *Mother Courage*, and if *US* began with Brechtian questions, it ended with non-Brechtian answers. By 1966 the possibilities of a politically adult drama in the Western democracies were subject to the laws of spectacle, and, in major theatres at least, the ensemble worked under, rather than with, directors and designers. The Brechtian model of a large ensemble working systematically according to a common ideology was certainly attractive to Brook, but the Royal Shakespeare Company could not provide such an ensemble. The question is whether a political theatre can survive without one.

US was singular and unrepeatable. I have put it forward as a director's oblique response to *Mother Courage*, and in that respect a lesson in inimitability. Other directors have been more straightforwardly influenced by Brecht, but none has set out so boldly to inhabit *Mother Courage*'s territory. It is the dialectical relationship between the two productions that makes comparison fruitful. A particular war is the ostensible subject of both, but where *US* was shockingly intimate, *Mother Courage* shocked by its distance. Brash theatricality and contrivance were employed by Brook to serve the purposes that Brecht had served by stealth. Not trusting his audience to make connections, Brook had his actors spell them out. But there is a penalty to pay for the abandonment of historicisation. *US* lost its necessary urgency when the Vietnam War ended. For me and for many of my generation, though, it was the established English theatre's unique demand that politicians should listen to the popular voice. With all its faults, of which the fundamental one was its substitution of sentiment for ideology, it contributed to the clamour for social reappraisal that seemed, briefly, to hold new hopes for democracy.

'MOTHER COURAGE' AND MUSIC THEATRE

Brecht has not recorded his reasons for including so many songs in *Mother Courage*. It is not a characteristic of the plays he was writing at that time. Simon Parmet, the Finnish composer with whom he first discussed his ideas for the music, found it impossible to meet Brecht's requirements without sounding like a watered-down version of Kurt Weill. 'I would like the numbers to be mechanical interludes', Brecht explained, 'with something of the sudden blaring out you get from slot machines in arcades.'[23] In the fulness of time, the compliant Dessau would do his best to meet the requirements. Weill, who would have met them more effectively, was already in America, where, in 1936, he had worked with Paul Green on a play of which Brecht might have been peripherally aware when he wrote *Mother Courage*. *Johnny Johnson* is a plea for pacifism, gently picaresque, more than a little naive, but certainly original. It covers the years from 1917 to 'today', and carries its very ordinary hero, much more of a simpleton than Schweyk or Mother Courage ever were, from small-town America to the battlefields of Europe on a personal mission to play his part in the war to end wars. 'I had put into it a lot of my abhorrence of war', wrote Green many years later, 'and made Johnny Johnson a kindly common-sense man against whom and through whom I might measure the violence of madness and hate.'[24] Amid the slaughter Johnny loses his faith in the good-will of those in power, and he initiates a deal with the German sol-diery to bring the war to an end through mutual non-cooperation with the generals. After a farcical scene involving laughing-gas and the Allied High Command, he impersonates a general and brings about a ceasefire. But the play does not end in wishful thinking.

Johnny is arrested, shipped back to New York and incarcerated in a psychiatric unit. There, serenely, he sets up a League of Nations among the inmates, and we last see him, after his release, selling toys on the streets of the city. Reviewing the production, which opened a troubled season for the Group Theatre in 1936, Marc Blitzstein wrote:

> Weill has practically added a new form to the musical theatre. It is not opera, although it partakes of the 'number' form of Mozart . . . This almost elementary, uninhibited use of music, seemingly careless, really profoundly sensitive, predicts something new for the theatre.[25]

The score is as busy as a cinematic sound-track, contradicting the mood of the drama almost as often as it heightens it, and although some of the songs spring directly from the narrative, not all do. *Johnny Johnson* is a fair reminder of the part Weill played in the development of Brecht's theories of theatre-music. It is, however, programmatically pacifist in a way that Brecht would have considered simple-minded. The Spanish Civil War was in a progress when *Johnny Johnson* opened on Broadway. Brecht's more robust response was *Senora Carrar's Rifles* (1937). That is not to deny *Johnny Johnson* an honourable place in the twentieth-century history of music theatre. It lacks the steadiness of purpose of *Mother Courage*, but it has significant features in common: it takes its hero on a picaresque journey into poverty and solitude against a background of war, its music is antithetical to the written text which it frequently alienates, and its scenes are arranged in epic fashion – in sequence rather than in consequence.

It is an old cause of concern that, whilst popular music is very popular indeed, popular theatre is almost a contradiction in terms. The musical was developed in order to bridge that gap, but not to challenge prejudice. Brecht's greater ambition was to greet the new audience of a knowledge-seeking age with a new kind of play, one in which music would not soften the harshness of the fiction. More controversially even than *The Threepenny Opera*, to which Weill applied the term, *Mother Courage* belongs to a *Zwischengattung* (an 'in-between genre'). Its songs maintain simultaneously a dialectical relationship with the spoken text and the listening audience. Joan Littlewood's heroic staging of *Oh, What A Lovely War!* (1963) was a spirited attempt to annex the musical and thematic territory of *Mother Courage*. With Brecht's association of war and business clearly in mind, Littlewood dared to present a musical extravaganza which aligned British patriotism with the bungling of big business; and she presented it to a Stratford East audience comprised in large part of that segment of the population whose grandfathers had made the supreme sacrifice in the Great War. It is only its starting-point (a historical war as social metaphor) and its reliance on a variety of *Verfremdungseffekte* that link *Oh, What A Lovely War!* to *Mother Courage*. Littlewood exonerates Mother Courages, placing the blame for mass-slaughter on politicians, generals and wealthy profiteers. There is a sequence early in Act 2 in which arms-manufacturers from Britain, France, Germany and America meet with a Swiss banker at a grouse-shoot. The dialogue is little more than a series of cartoon-captions – speeches written to give voice to George Grosz's grotesque capitalists. It is not from such people that we hear in *Mother Courage*. *Oh, What A Lovely War!* excuses the very people whom Brecht makes complicit. It mounts an attack on those in power, but its effect is to confirm the powerlessness of those they oppress.

The peculiar style of music theatre exemplified by *Mother Courage* has been variously developed during the last quarter of the century. Brecht's emphatic use of songs within a play that had no obvious call for them was a liberating precedent for many of the radical theatre groups whose work expressed the political optimism of the youthful years around 1968. Strangely, though, audiences seldom associate *Mother Courage* with a music theatre. Donald Soule, whose recollection of the two German actresses who first played Mother Courage I cited earlier, could not remember whether or not Therese Giehse sang, and that is not untypical. To an extent that has proved hard to imitate, *Mother Courage* incorporates its songs in its debate. British playwrights – John McGrath in *Yobbo Nowt* (1975), Caryl Churchill in *Vinegar Tom* (1976), Edward Bond in *Restoration* (1981) – have been particularly alert to the possibilities of the new music theatre. As Brecht was well aware, this new theatre looked back to the ancient foundations of dramatic performance. It is probable that, in order to survive, the theatre of the future will strengthen its ties with music. But music is an overwhelming art. A theatre that wishes to maintain open access to the integrity of its own discourses whilst inviting musical interventions may find itself harking back to the precedent of *Mother Courage*.

AFTER 'MOTHER COURAGE'

I turn finally to a consideration of some of the ways in which *Mother Courage* has resonated in the recent history of the drama, outside the boundaries of the music theatre. Brecht's own *Schweyk in the Second World War* may be taken as a starting-point. I have already referred to Brecht's own description of *Schweyk* as a counter-play (*Gegenstück*) to *Mother Courage*. In so far as any individual can, Schweyk makes a fool of the war by playing the fool in it. He insults the war by not taking it seriously, picking up his occasional profits by chance rather than set policy, entering, as he says, the black-market business in the same way as Pontius Pilate entered the Creed. His cunning is effective because it is indistinguishable from idiocy, and his enforced participation in the war changes neither his behaviour nor his idiom. Mother Courage has some of the same speech-patterns, and this has tempted some actresses to play her as a shifty exploiter of war. During rehearsals for the 1978 production at the Theater am Schiffbauerdamm, Kupke pressed Gisela May to abandon her 'Schweyk-May-Brecht-talk' and replace it with a 'May-Courage-Brecht-talk'.[26] It is a stylistic distinction of some subtlety, since Schweyk and Mother Courage are about equally given to Bavarian colloquialisms in their war-dialogue. Meaning belongs to people, though, not to words; and when Mother Courage utters her unpalatable opinions she does not have her tongue in her cheek. She takes her war very seriously indeed:

> They call me Courage, sergeant, because when I saw ruin staring me in the face, I drove out of Riga through cannon fire with fifty loaves of bread in my wagon. They were getting moldy, it was high time, I had no choice. (*p. 137*)

At the end of her play Mother Courage is still in hot pursuit of the war. At the end of his Schweyk is lost in a snowstorm, and we do not believe for a moment that he is trying to find his way to Stalingrad. 'Let's go home', he advises the equally lost Hitler in the savagely farcical Epilogue. 'Here we are nowhere.' Mother Courage has the wit to recognise that her own motives are the same as those of the generals in a bourgeois war. Schweyk has the wit to steer clear of motives altogether.

Many years intervened between Brecht's writing of *Schweyk* and its inclusion in the repertoire of the Berliner Ensemble. The play did not harmonise with the principles of socialist realism, with which the Ensemble was increasingly trammelled in the years immediately following Brecht's death. An apposite example of the company's nervous reaction is the staging of Helmut Baierl's *Frau Flinz* in 1961. Frau Flinz is Mother Courage transformed by the touch of East German socialism. She learns from her mistakes, and achieves the resolution to adapt to the demands of the new society. Since Helene Weigel played the title role, the alternative proposed by Baierl had an additional symbolic dimension; but there is a fundamental evasion of Marxist dialectic that makes *Frau Flinz* a tepid *Gegenstück*. I am reminded of the eighteenth-century stage direction recalled by George Colman the Younger: 'The Miser leans against the wall and grows generous.'[27] Frau Flinz's change of heart, the consequence of a socialist epiphany, lacks the political clout of Mother Courage's unfaltering commitment to the values of bourgeois capitalism. Baierl may have gratified his paymasters by his portrayal of a modern Mother Courage who leans against the wall and becomes socialist, but his is a minimal contribution to ideological discourse. Twenty years before Baierl wrote *Frau Flinz*, Brecht had noted in his journal:

> it will probably be well nigh impossible to demand that reality be presented in such a way that it can be mastered, without pointing to the contradictory, ongoing character of conditions, events, figures, for unless you recognise the dialectical nature of reality it cannot be mastered.[28]

The argument led him to the dramaturgically decisive conclusion that 'the mysteries of the world are not solved, they are demonstrated'.

In *Mother Courage* Brecht provides the evidence but withholds the verdict. It might reasonably be argued that this is a characteristic of all great drama, but Brecht's demand on the audience is peculiarly insistent. The impact of the Berliner Ensemble's production was felt by playwrights in all the countries to which it toured. For Arthur Adamov in France it led to a radical change of direction – away from nightmarish absurdism to a concern with politico-economic realities. *Paolo Paoli*, staged by Roger Planchon in 1957, was Adamov's idiosyncratic response to *Mother Courage*. Deftly and improbably threading Marxist dialectic into the dramaturgy of French farce, Adamov exposes the economic priorities of French participation in World War I through the machinations of his two principal characters, one of whom trades in butterflies and the other in feathers. Despite its proclaimed debt to *Mother Courage*, Adamov's play has no discernible likeness to Brecht's. Its battles are fought indoors in a context of household trivia and adultery. The truth is, rather, that both Adamov and Planchon were working off the excitement of *Mother Courage*, and their collaboration was of great significance in the importation of Brecht into the French theatre.

British playwrights have been more cagey than Adamov in acknowledging the influence of Brecht, and yet one of them, John

Arden, is the author of the only modern play that may confidently be said to rival *Mother Courage* in its emotional range and dialectical awareness. I find if difficult to believe that *Serjeant Musgrave's Dance* would have been written were it not for *Mother Courage*. That is not to say that Arden's play is modelled on Brecht's; rather that Arden's imagination was fired by sparks from *Mother Courage*. Early in his career, Arden selected *Mother Courage* as the play he would most like to have written, but in 1966 – seven years after the première of *Serjeant Musgrave's Dance* – he assured an interviewer:

> I don't copy Brecht; I don't use him as a model. After I had started writing plays I decided that Brecht was inspired by the same sort of early drama that was interesting me: the rather conventionalised plays of the European Middle Ages, the Elizabethan writers and various exotic styles such as the Japanese and Chinese theatre.[29]

Arden was by some way the most thoughtful of the new wave of British playwrights at the end of the 1950s. The puzzled and generally hostile critical reception of the original production of *Serjeant Musgrave's Dance* at the Royal Court spoke for a theatre that was suspicious of intellect. Harold Hobson, for example, was magisterially insistent to readers of the *Sunday Times*:

> It is time someone reminded our advanced dramatists that the principal function of the theatre is to give pleasure. It is not the principal function of the theatre to strengthen peace, to improve morality or to establish a good social system. Churches, international associations and political parties already exist for those purposes. It is the duty of the theatre, not to make men better, but to render them harmlessly happy.[30]

Like Brecht, Arden sets himself up as an adversary of this narcotic trade. Like Brecht's, his historicising is designed to provoke a rethinking of contemporary values and to challenge common perceptions of power.

Serjeant Musgrave and his three companions arrive in the snowbound northern town like developed versions of the two recruiters in the opening scene of *Mother Courage*. It is not until late in the play that we learn for sure that theirs is not a recruiting mission, or that the miners can be confident that it is not a strike-breaking one. What then emerges is that Serjeant Musgrave owns the ideology and will not share it with his three subordinates. It is the intensity of his mission that governs the action of the play, per-meating it with a sense of mysterious purpose and special occasion that is entirely absent from *Mother Courage*. Indeed, *Serjeant Musgrave's Dance* comes close to adhering to the Aristotelean unities of time, place and action. It is in the visual shaping of the play – its 'scenic writing' – that Arden most clearly reveals his debt to *Mother Courage*. His Introduction to the published text insists:

> Scenery must be sparing – only those pieces of architecture, furniture and properties actually used in the action need be present: and they should be thoroughly realistic, so that the audience sees a selection from the details of everyday life rather than a generalised impression of the whole of it.

What is being proposed is a reproduction of the visual and sensory impact of the Berliner Ensemble's *Mother Courage*. This is the realism of the early modern street-ballads, with which *Mother Courage*, too, is in touch: 'red uniforms in a black-and-white coalfield'.[31] And Arden is as uninterested as Brecht and the bal-ladeers in details of psychology. It is not motives but events that *Serjeant Musgrave's Dance* deals in. Its world is violent, and its deaths as cruel and incidental as those of Mother Courage's children. Arden uses violence as a metaphor for power, and Musgrave's defiance, like Mother Courage's strategy for survival, is ultimately exposed as compliance with the exploiters. Eilif's war-dance in Scene 2 of *Mother Courage* is an obscene postlude to casual slaughter: Musgrave's shamanistic dance of death in the market-place is an obscene prelude to casual slaughter. In the real world of both plays the casual and the convenient are all too often synonymous, and power remains in the hands of the powerful.

No modern playwright with a concern for political ideologies has been untouched by Brecht, but the symbiotic relationship of *Serjeant Musgrave's Dance* and *Mother Courage* is unique. Musgrave stands over his three soldiers like a heavy father, and the unit of four resonates with the family group of Mother Courage. In each case, the obsession of the 'parent' leads to the destruction of the group: small deaths in a world that scarcely notices. Without copying its methods, and perhaps beyond his consciousness, Arden apprehended *Mother Courage* and transfigured it. 'To watch a play by Arden,' as Frances Gray has observed, 'or to participate in one, is to engage in a debate about theatre – what it is for, and whom it is for.'[32] As in Brecht's plays, the debate is provoked by a deliberate contradiction of expectation, a making strange of dramatic material which the audience might otherwise find reassuringly familiar.

Serjeant Musgrave's Dance is not precisely located in place or time, although its reference is clearly to Britain's recent imperial and industrial history. Like Brecht, Arden has created stage-images to indicate the impact of militarism on ordinary lives. A question insistently raised by both *Mother Courage* and *Serjeant Musgrave's Dance* is: 'How long will the dominated continue to capitulate to the value systems of the dominators?' It is a question that has been raised with renewed urgency in Europe by the horrific conflict among the nation-states of the artificially created country of Yugoslavia. Here, as in the Thirty Years War, towns and cities have been casually turned into battlefields, atrocities committed in the name of religion, citizens suddenly made soldiers through the mere accident of residence. For Giorgio Strehler in Milan, these events have lifted *Mother Courage* into new currency. Strehler was one, perhaps the very best, of the then-young directors whose ideas were still forming when the Berliner Ensemble toured *Mother Courage*. Since then, during his long career as artistic director of the Piccolo Teatro in Milan, he has directed several of Brecht's plays, but never *Mother Courage*. Never, that is, until the summer of 1996, when he chose to open the company's new theatre with a production of *Madre Coraggio di Sarajevo*. Franco Fortini's version of the play was less a radical transformation than a repointing, but Strehler's determination to enforce the contemporaneity of the whole project was signalled in a series of public readings – in the weeks immediately preceding the première in Milan – across Italy. The first of these took place on 28 June 1996 in the Via D'Amelio in Palermo, outside the house where the Mafia had assassinated their prosecuting judge. Borsellino's widow and his mother were in the audience, and Strehler, who was unable to be there, had arranged for the delivery to Maria Borsellino (the Mother Courage of Palermo) of a bunch of red roses. It was in her house, *this* house, that the execution of her brave son had occurred. There is very little of Brecht in the Mediterranean flamboyance of Strehler's gesture, but the purpose of these public readings was very serious indeed. Strehler advertised the Palermo event with a short statement:

> This is not a spectacle, it is a symbol. In defence of our culture and as a fundamental act on behalf of our country: an act which speaks to our tragic capacity to continue to make war and to live with war. War that is a sign of the bankruptcy of humanity.[33]

The reading was led by Giulia Lazzarini, costumed as a penurious citizen of Sarajevo, and accompanied by the Dessau score played by a full orchestra. Twenty-one students from the studio of the Piccolo Teatro read the other parts. It was not Brecht's play, nor even Franco Fortini's, that Strehler was most urgent to display – it was the need to *do* something *now*.

It is not only Strehler who has recognised, in the wake of the Balkan conflict, a new currency in *Mother Courage*. In Graham Ackroyd's *The Forests Are Burning*,[34] Rena battles with and for her extended family in a besieged town with a mixture of blindness and cunning that recalls Mother Courage herself. The young Macedonian playwright, Jugoslav Petrovski, provides in *Porcelain*

Vase a montage of episodes of casual brutality that reflects the unseen reality of Eilif's military exploits. But the direct links between *Mother Courage* and these two plays are matters of debate. They are not so in the case of the Slovenian Dusan Jovanović's *The Puzzle of Courage*.[35]

Jovanović is characteristically concerned with the theatre's hold on reality. In *The Puzzle of Courage*, the actress Irena, rehearsing the part of Mother Courage, is brought face to face with a mother widowed in the wars in former Yugoslavia. The play is in three movements: Courage, Fear and Something Else. It is a play which strays further and further into enigma as it progresses, but the first movement is a critique of the efficacy of Brecht's *Mother Courage*. It culminates in Irena's smashing of the property wagon. This is the twenty-third in a sequence of disconnected episodes, many of them set metatheatrically on the stage. The first episode discovers the forty-year-old Irena in bed with the director of *Mother Courage* and already expressing an anxiety that permeates the play: 'on stage, I always know what I'm feeling; in life, never!' How, then – and Jovanović is making the point that the question follows logically – will she play Mother Courage? What happens to Brecht's play when it is performed in a real theatre of war and with the central role played by an actress who doesn't know where she stands? The director's answer is bland. Irena will play the part 'as required'. In the second episode, alone on stage with the play's assembled properties, Irena reminds herself of the need not to try to please the audience nor to try to excel those who have played the part before her: 'I must be reconciled with the bare reality and with the effects of bare fact . . . No fear, just courage! But who'll help me?' The crisis in her life has been precipitated by the professional requirement that she play, *here* and *now*, a role which demands clarity. As an actress, Irena needs answers. For the director it is sufficient to pose questions. He tells the cast (episode four) that Mother Courage's concern that her family should do well in a world that is doing badly is 'a typical bourgeois illusion of the world', that socialism has in the 1990s been quashed by Fascism, and that 'there are no more people like Brecht', concluding that:

> The question with which we are faced is: have we all capitulated?
> And the other question: are we not all, each in our own way, and in ourselves, only one of the faces of Mother Courage?

But how does that help the actress of Mother Courage? Irena takes her problems to a psychotherapist.

Jovanović either refuses or fails to resolve the function of Olga, the psychotherapist, within the play. Her reading of the character of Brecht's Mother Courage is Stanislavskian. This is a person, she explains to Irena (episode five), who exhibits none of the symptoms normal in those who have experienced the loss of loved ones; and when she comes to analyse Irena's behaviour during the course of the play's second movement, she does so in terms that are marginal to Jovanović's play and irrelevant to Brecht's – Irena is 'trying to escape from the role for some strange reason'; the cocker spaniel she buys is an attempt to replace Swiss Cheese (is that compatible with escaping from the role?); she has 'buried the role of Mother Courage because it can't be played'. Even if these were psychological truths, it would be hard to define their purpose. Olga seems sporadically to employ Mother Courage as Freud employed Oedipus – as a character exemplary of a complex. But the psychological fiction lacks the conviction of the 'real-life' character of Marija.

Marija is brought by the director to meet the acting company during the sixth episode of the first movement. From then on, she inadvertently competes with Irena for the role of Mother Courage. Marija married out of her religion, and has seen her husband killed by her own people in this religious war. Once the family dealt in iron; now, she and her two surviving children beg for a living. For the director, Marija is a sensational model for Mother Courage; for Irena, from the start and increasingly, she is yet another block to performance. Irena at first resolves to acknowledge her fears but not to play them – to allow the audience to guess what is invisible. But the director (episode nine) is determinedly Brechtian:

> You have to be cynical, and the audience sentimental . . . It's crucial that you portray contradictions . . . There's no courage, she's an animal. Just instinct, no psychology.

Irena is left to battle alone with her neurotic involvement in the efforts of Mother Courage–Marija to 'live this lousy war through'. Her problems are compounded in episode eleven, when the actors pay a Stanislavsky-style study-visit to the stable in which Marija and her children are squatting. Dino, the crippled son, is pleased to have an audience for his story. He was shot by one of his own side, fooling with a gun. Of the fifty-three dead in his division, thirty-nine were killed by their own colleagues. He will be twenty-three next birthday. The best thing in his life now is the cordless telephone awarded in compensation by the state. Unfortunately, though, he has no one to phone. He lets it be known (the family are beggars by trade) that an electric wheelchair would improve his life, and the director arranges for him to receive one previously used for an O'Neill play. Issues of motherhood begin to crowd in on the childless Irena, whose anxieties are exacerbated by the attentions of the twelve-year-old daughter Katica. It is a pressure that increases over the rest of the play.

It is not until the twentieth episode of the first movement that Irena and Marija have their first direct confrontation. Having recognised that material benefits might follow, Marija has welcomed her Mother Courage role. Irena is morally affronted. 'Who made you into Mother Courage?', she asks. 'You did!' This is a fair point, but Marija is unrepentant. Taking advantage of her sudden prominence, she has established a knitting workshop and staffed it with victims of the war: 'I knew it would only work if the thing was presented as a humanitarian action . . . I got the wool free. That was the jackpot.' You would expect a Mother Courage to exhibit this kind of business acumen, and to counter Irena's outrage with an attack on the theatrical profession: 'If you aren't ashamed to use my grief for your shitty theatre, you've no need to be ashamed now!' For Irena, the knowledge that a performance of *Mother Courage* might be read as exploitation is a step towards breakdown. Irena's decline is traced through the final three episodes of the first movement. Her extraordinary encounters with Marija's children increase her disorientation. Her histrionic training is in psychology, but the peasant world of Marija and her family is both unlovely and unsubtle. Is it Jovanović's intention to bring Brecht to book for overrating the native wit of the Mother Courages and their families? They operate, certainly, at a level beneath Irena's understanding. She gets nowhere in her attempt to understand why Katica wants to be a nun or a whore when she grows up. All Katica knows is that neither whores nor nuns have children. In the penultimate episode, alone with Dino, Irena has abandoned her attempts to understand. She lets Dino suck her nipples and then sinks back beside him to light a joint. It is in the next, and final, episode of the first movement that she returns to the theatre to smash Mother Courage's wagon. There is certainly an implication that Brecht has got it wrong, if not for his own time, then crucially for Jovanović's.

The next movement (Fear) is interspersed with scenes that may be memories plucked from Irena's past or that may be her dreams/nightmares. The play is passing into shapelessness in accordance with Jovanović's apprehension of the realities of war. In the second episode Irena makes a new discovery about Marija. She has gone into the provisions business, running the Barbecue Lamb with Brecht's Cook. Dino's wheelchair has been dismantled so that the spit can be electrically operated, and his cordless telephone is in use to take orders. 'There's nothing to say you've got to be poor', says Marija, and Irena wonders, 'Is this the meaning of courage?' This startlingly theatrical episode ends with the entry of an abusive sergeant who treats Dino, no longer able to conceal his drug-addiction, with particular savagery. When his insults turn to threats, the

Cook shoots him in the back. A fictional character, Brecht's invention, commits a 'real' murder which is, of course, a fiction. The critique of *Mother Courage* is dissipated. Instead, the play concludes in metatheatrical speculations. In so far as a dialogue with Brecht is maintained, it is a debate whose outcome is predetermined by Jovanović's desolate postmodernism. There is no political hope in *The Puzzle of Courage* – no personal hope either – and Jovanović's bleak verdict seems to be that *Mother Courage* can no longer speak to his society.

It may be that this is a peculiarly European verdict. It is not one with which to conclude a study of the performance history of one of the twentieth century's greatest plays. I turn instead to Viv Gardner's joyous account of a third-world production of *Mother Courage*: one of the rare occasions on which the play has been produced in an African country. The account of *Maama Nalukalala Ne'zzadde Lye* is not in my words, but in those of Viv Gardner. She was there: I was not.

*   *   *

Uganda is Mother Courage's land. The soil is red, an extraordinary deep rust red. The road from Entebbe airport to Kampala is a red slash through the fecund green of banana, frangipani and bougainvillaea. The coffin-makers display their wares at the roadside, as do the welders of cars and gates, the sellers of tomatoes, yams, bananas and Coca-Cola. Outside Kampala cars seem relatively rare but bicycles are not, bicycles laden with children, chickens, ten-foot poles, water-carriers, bananas and Coca-Cola.

On stage, Maama Nalukalala's cart is not a bicycle but an ancient railway-yard truck on a huge lorry-axle, surmounted by a bedframe to create a 'tent' whose walls are rattan blinds and the goods that she has acquired. In Scene 7, when Maama Nalukalala is at the height of her success, the cart seems as high as it is long with booty: booty that will be looted by silent figures during the progress of Scene 9. On stage too is the earth that is so characteristic of the southern areas of Uganda. A rectangle of red fills the playing area, creating a stage within a stage. During the performance the soil becomes churned and rutted, and the torn polythene beneath it is dragged through by the wheels of the cart and the feet of the actors. The proscenium frame of the National Theatre is breached by an apron built of rough planking. The back wall of the stage is an unforgiving concrete grey. Downstage on the apron sit six musicians in white *kanzu*. Centre-back is the cart. The image is familiar. A woman braced proudly on the front platform of the cart, in front of her a younger women, seated. Two young men in the wooden yoke of the truck. There is an eerie wailing blast, joined by a peppershot of drums and then a rhythmic, slurred scraping on plastic. Gradually the voices of Maama Nalukalala and the actors take up the song. Dumb Kattrin 'sings' by breathing across the top of a Coca-Cola bottle. The horn is an eight-foot funeral horn, the drums a mixture of native drums and plastic-bottle crates. Then, with visibly necessary effort, Eilif and Swiss Cheese press forward in the yoke, and after some seconds the cart begins to roll forward.

This was the opening to a production of *Mother Courage and Her Children*, performed in Uganda nine years after the end of the civil wars. It was the first authorised production of a Brecht play in an African language, Laganda, the language of the Baganda district of Uganda. It is not difficult to understand why the Ugandans have been drawn to *Mother Courage*, but it was difficult for me, totally innocent and ignorant about Africa, to imagine how much this production would show me the play alive – shorn of the dead hand of classicism and canonisation that has dogged my experience of Brecht in Britain. It was staged at the National Theatre in Kampala in 1995, and in the month that Uganda celebrated its Independence Day (9 October) with the promulgation of a new constitution:

> Sunday, 8th October. Ate at the Sheritan [*sic*]. On walking up the hill
> to the hotel, fireworks from the roof began, sending a number of the

twilight girls running for cover. Who they were brought a smile but why they ran was yet another reminder of what the whole population has been through in recent years.[36]

It is impossible not to be reminded of the twenty years of dictatorship and civil war, terrorism and censorship that all but destroyed the political, economic and cultural infrastructure of Uganda under the regimes of Nelson Obote (1966–71 and 1980–85) and Idi Amin (1971–9), and the chaotic, short-lived governments of Yusef Lule (1979) and Godfrey Binaisa (1979–80). Joined to the back of the National Theatre is the national radio station. The walls are pockmarked with bullet-holes, showing where successive forces had fought for control of 'the voice of the people'. Towering above the theatre is an extraordinary building, housing one of the government ministries. Perhaps twenty storeys high, it is framed in a tracery of black ironwork. When completed, the iron was covered in bronzed glass – all shot away in the street-fighting in Kampala over the years. The car park in front of the National Theatre is pot-holed, and supports not only the taxi-rank but also a rubbish tip and a family of 'homeless' Buganda. One of the modernist streetlamps leans at a crazy angle, and the ever-present, carrion-eating Maribou storks – reputed, like the vultures in the garden of the Sheraton Hotel, to have arrived only during Amin's period of power – cruise overhead. Some of the older members of the cast of *Maama Nalukalala* had been working with Byron Kawadwa, playwright and director of the National Theatre, when he and five of his actors were taken from the theatre and murdered by Amin's men in March 1977. The theatre itself has not, apparently, been refurbished, despite a proposed commitment from Japan in 1990 to finance a renovation, since the British built it for the expatriate community in 1959. The present government's limited resources for theatre work have been channelled into educational theatre, above all for those involved in the campaign against AIDS.

This production was funded by the British Council. It had its origin in workshops jointly conducted in Kampala in 1994 by the

Ugandan Theatre Guild and the Royal Court Theatre. Working with an English translation of the text, the African actors encountered some difficulty. English English is not Ugandan English. It sounded too formal, too stilted. It lacked the flexibility, the ironic tone of Brecht's German. One group translated their scene into Laganda – and from there the idea grew. Joanita Bewulira-Wandera produced a performance script which clearly caught the Brechtian flavour. The company that was formed for the project was unique. It was made up of members of the 400 or so amateur and semi-professional theatre companies – there being no fully professional theatre companies in Uganda; such distinctions are inappropriate there – that have sprung up in the Kampala region since the end of hostilities in 1986, of students and staff from Makerere University's Music, Dance and Drama Department (MDD) and from the Theatre Guild, and of four British professionals. The production brought together, then, academics, actors accustomed to working from a text, popular improvisational performers like Joseph Musoke (the Cook) and 'the John Cleese of Kampala'[37] Charles Senkubuge (the General), and a television presenter, Irene Kulabako (Yvette). Despite this, the acting company worked seamlessly. What they all had in common, in addition to their commitment to the project, was a presentational performance style that is foreign to most European actors. Time and time again, in watching the rehearsals and in the performance, I was reminded of Brecht's essay 'The Street Scene' and of his poem 'On Everyday Theatre'. With a strong background in non-verbal theatre and dance, Ugandan actors are comfortably physically expressive. In Scene 6, Maama Nalukalala (Professor Rose Mbowa from Makerere University MDD), pairing and packing away socks, with ambiguous carelessness but tangible sexuality turns her backside to the Chaplain. There is no vulgarity or apology in this middle-aged woman's gesture. She skilfully completes the inventory of her goods, discusses the death of Tilly – and inflames the Chaplain. The Chaplain's violent and rhythmic attack on the log later in the scene, as he warns Nalukalala about his rival the Cook, is explained in this physical moment. When Maama Nalukalala walks off behind the wagon with an easy roll of the hips, this is compared and contrasted in the memory with an identical move by Yvette in Scene 3, when she crosses the stage with the acquired commercial sashay of the prostitute.

Physical gesture is never extraneous. Maama Nalukalala slaps the heels of her hands together then makes two fists that she holds close to her head to express frustration in a way that a similar gesture in European theatre – the slapping of the thigh, perhaps – would seem extravagant, melodramatic. There is a vocal gesture of contempt or disapproval, inimitable by a *musungu* (white/foreigner), somewhere between a 'tut-tut' and a suck of the teeth, that was used to great effect on both sides of the proscenium. Semwogere Wankalibo as the Chaplain hangs his head and makes this sound over Maama Nalukalala's fatal obduracy in bargaining with Yvette over Swiss Cheese's ransom. Two women in the audience use it as Maama Nalukalala sings her lullaby over the dead body of her daughter, having learned nothing.

The Kampala theatre was, as Brecht required, 'vivid, earthy theatre fed by the daily human contact/That takes place on the street',[38] full of 'virtuosity, imagination, humour and fellow feeling'.[39] But it was also capable of great power and complexity. In Scene 2, Eilif sings his 'Song of the Fishwife and the Soldier' and dances for the General. MDD student Abubaker Kawenje (Eilif) is over six feet tall, with the body of a man and the open expression of a child. He turns to the front, holds his *panga* away from his body, and performs a war dance as he sings – a dance that is simultaneously athletic, beautiful and awesome. This is no African folk dance. In khaki singlet and trousers, with a faintly ridiculous straw hat on his head, the image of young Rwandan soldiers is too fresh for this to be either quaint or funny. For the Ugandans, a similar memory of young Ugandans (and of the Generals who led them) is only ten years old. As he turns to his General, the latter – a short man in a slightly too-tight uniform jacket – smiling nervously and waving a

Plate 10 Kattrin (Sylvia Namutebi) and Mother Courage (Rose Mbowa) pause in front of the dilapidated and depleted wagon in Scene 10 of the 1995 production at the National Theatre in Kampala, directed by Jane Collins and Jessica Kaahwa.

convivial glass at Eilif in encouragement, shifts backwards in his chair until it meets the proscenium arch, threatening to trap the General in the trajectory of his hero's weapon. A little man delighting in, yet fearful of, the demon he has unleashed. The scene is both terrifying and funny. The dance is performed for both the General and the audience, but the scene is framed by a performance style that is clearly outward-turning, showing both men to be ridiculous, but powerful in different ways.

The narrative, oral and musical traditions of African culture, deliberately employed by directors Jane Collins and Jessica Kaahwa, also appear natural Brechtian tools. The music was an African response to Dessau's score, a collaborative venture involving all the musicians, and the three musical directors (Jackson Kamutu, Salongo Sennoga and Stephen Warbeck) in particular. The dramatic flexibility of the drums and other percussion instruments, both purpose-made and improvised, was crucial to the dynamic of the performance. The absence of any melodic instrument apart from the actor's voice meant that there was always a tension between the singer and the music. It was without a hint of sentimentality. The music and musicians worked both as part of the action on the stage and as a commentary on the action.[40] They were part of the story-telling framing of the performance, along with the title-captions for each scene, which were delivered as 'story' with commentary and reaction from the rest of the company. A device that would appear false and self-consciously theatrical in Britain was entirely natural in an auditorium where the audience comment on the dramatic action amongst themselves and to the stage, where women bring their babies and their crochet, where the occasional bored young man leaves without apology or recrimination. Brecht was aware that 'a deeply engrained habit leads the theatre-goer to pick out the more emotional utterances of the characters and overlook everything else' (p. 341). This is not true of the Ugandan audience. Their response is disconcerting to a European. They laugh at moments and at performances guaranteed to wring tears from a British audience – Kattrin's death produced laughter, gasps and muted 'Ay-Ay-Ay-Ays'. They rarely express approval through applause, even at the end of a performance. It was not simply that this production of *Mother Courage* was funnier than any I have seen, though it was, it was that the spectators were engaged, but in a way that I have never experienced.

Above all this was an audience that listened and heard. There was no need to transfer the action to Uganda. This was Brecht's play about the Thirty Years War; Bavaria remained Bavaria, Swiss Cheese, Swiss Cheese (though engagingly to the European ear pronounced 'Swissee Cheesee'). There is too much in the play that is acutely pertinent to the Ganda and their immediate past. For them, the play's discussion of war is not 'a timeless abstraction' (p. 341). You could hear the audience's approval of Maama Nalukalala's condemnation of the virtues needed under a bad *kabaka* (king) or general in

Scene 2. In reading about Uganda's post-colonial history one is struck by the parallels with the Thirty Years War. Two wars that spanned several generations. Wars whose origin lay in a complex matrix of ethnic (Swedish, Finnish, Bohemian, Polish/Baganda, Acholi, Banyankole, Banyoro etc.), religious (Protestant, Catholic/ Muslim, Protestant, Catholic, Hindu[41]) and economic causes. Both wars occurred at a time of major historical shifts; the Thirty Years War at the intersection of feudal and capitalist societies, the Ugandan wars in the aftermath of British colonial rule. Both wars ebbed and flowed over vast areas, and 'victory' switched sides in a similarly fluid manner. The Europe of the play and present-day Uganda both have large peasant populations for whom the loss of an ox is a real threat. And, as the Minister for Gender and Culture said on the first night, 'We all have our Maama Nalukalalas.'

The play frequently touched the lives of the cast too. Rehearsals were punctuated by stories of the atrocities and absurdities experienced during the war.[42] They were told unsensationally, simply as confirmation of Brecht's story. Even the younger members had memories. During the discussion of how Christine Nanjobe should handle the Peasant Woman's prayer in Scene 11 – in a 'wretchedly routine fashion' born of repeated abuse, as Brecht suggests in his notes,[43] or with sincerity, fear etc. – Charles Malekwa, who played a soldier in this scene, told of how he remembered his aunt praying every night, habitually but with genuine belief, at each possible entry point to the house, asking for God to bless the spot and prevent the soldiers breaking in. Everyone had both an understanding and a respect for the three responses in that scene to the threat from the soldiers – the collaboration of the old peasant (Sem Wankalibo), belated support for Kattrin from the young peasant (Evans Kiyingi), and Kattrin's own 'heroic' stand. Everyone too recognised the significance in the opening scene of the Sergeant's barked order, 'N' jo hapa sassa' (You, come here now), in Kiswahili rather than Laganda – the language of the occupying Tanzanian army which liberated Uganda from Idi Amin. The design solution for Scene 1 also came from the cast's experience – it was obvious to Joseph Walugembe and Paul Bakibinga, who played the Recruiting Officer and the Sergeant, that the soldiers should be at one of the many road blocks improvised from tyres, crates and planks. The tyres became an essential part of the staging, forming the base for flagpoles, crosses and tent-poles.

The staging of the production cast a new light on Brecht's poem, 'Weigel's Props'. The designers, Michael Mpyangu and Michael Pavelka, selected with care equal to Weigel's the setting and props 'to accompany [the] characters across the stage'. The markets were scoured, improbable bargains struck – an aged wood-seller, dressed in *kanzu*, cap and American forces tunic, agreed to hire out his jacket (for the General) for the price of a new one (and to sell some timber into the bargain) – bribes paid at road blocks and a judge bearded in his chambers for the bamboo growing in his garden. All the props acquired were 'selected for age, function and beauty',[44] but the beauty was that of an orange plastic jerry-can, already cut in half to make a bowl, in which the Chaplain could wash glasses; an assortment of rusty kitchen-knives for Sylvia Namutebi's Kattrin to clean and sharpen; an enormously heavy canteen-turned-cash-box, made of olive-coloured metal, for Swiss Cheese (Jack Serunkuma); a wheelbarrow as a gun-base (the vendor kept the wheel so that the designers had to buy another separately: one can see similar barrows all over the country, 'parked up' without their wheels for security reasons). The 'beauty of use' found in a country like Uganda lies as much in the ingenuity with which the people recycle objects as in the objects themselves. When the designers were unable to borrow or hire any guns – an understandable restriction in present Ugandan circumstances – they constructed the gun that was used to shoot Kattrin from an old Pattern 93 stage-lantern, *circa* 1930. The resulting strange and cumbersome contraption, mounted on the wheelbarrow, was somehow more suggestive of destructive power than any real weapon could have been.

The props and furniture also served a gestic function. It

emerged in rehearsal that there was a clear etiquette in seating, determined by status – male over female, age over youth, bourgeois over peasant – that dictated the height of the seat off the ground. Thus, for the second part of Scene 3, when Maama Nalukalala, Kattrin, Swiss Cheese and the Chaplain sat eating, their seats were chosen with great care. As the youngest and a female, Kattrin sat on a mat, Swiss Cheese on a crate, and Maama Nalukalala on her own 'throne', an ochre-coloured car seat found at the back of the theatre. The Chaplain, despite his gender and superior social standing, was made to squat on a crate lower than Swiss Cheese's and, of course, than Nalukalala's throne. Other gestic points involving the use of props were more serendipitous. There was an extraordinary moment when Maama Nalukalala produced a small plastic lid, the top from something long since lost, now full of ash, and began wiping it on to Kattrin's face to make her unattractive to the victorious Catholic soldiers. Against Sylvia Namutebi's dark skin, the ashes showed both as ashes – a ritual gesture of mourning – and as a whitening agent: Kattrin's Ugandan beauty being despoiled by being 'made *musungu*'.

The only time there was any real divergence of opinion between the Ugandan and British members of the company was over the property chickens, which provoked several exchanges about Brecht and realism. The capon that Maama Nalukalala sells to the Cook in Scene 2 was, like Weigel's, 'hand-picked'. The problem for the Ugandans was that it was dead. Ugandans do not buy and sell dead chickens. The problem for the British was the need to kill the chicken on stage before it was plucked. In this instance sentiment won over realism.[45] Two live chickens *were* bought, but as cart-dressing for Maama Nalukalala's glory years. (Being highly mobile, they were given the only dressing-room and the careful attention of the stage-manager, Michael Muhumuza, despite the fact that they were hardly 'good props', as they could not be seen on stage in their wicker basket. It was suggested during the technical rehearsal that they should be painted white, but the idea was lost in the chaos that ensued when a tropical storm interrupted proceedings.)

However, deluges were almost the least of the company's problems, and it is partly the context in which this production was nurtured that makes its success so extraordinary to me, a cosseted European. Brecht wrote:

> Now, after the great war, life goes on in our ruined cities, but it is
> a different life, the life of different or differently composed groups,
> guided or thwarted by new surroundings, new because so much has
> been destroyed. The great heaps of rubble are piled on the city's
> invaluable substructure, the water and drainage pipes, the gas mains
> and electric cables. Even the large building that has remained intact is
> affected by the damage and rubble around it . . . All this is reflected in
> art, for our way of thinking is part of our way of living.   (*p. 334*)

As I write, it is ten years since Yoweri Museveni and the National Resistance Army defeated Obote's UNLA and seized power. Museveni was sworn in as President on 29 January 1986. Since then Uganda has achieved a large measure of stability. There is a conspicuous reduction in ethnic tension, though some problems persist in the northern areas bordering Sudan. But Uganda remains a 'desperately poor country with an abundance of political, economic and social problems'.[46] The great piles of rubble still lie in the streets of Kampala.

Throughout the rehearsal period, the European members of the company received constant reminders of the day-to-day circumstances in which their Ugandan fellows lived. Hospital vigils were commonplace – AIDS, malaria, measles, road accidents. Funerals were one or two a week. Salongo Sennoga, the musical director, was missing for many days – raising money for his children's school fees and mobilising the parents of other children who had been sent home because they had been unable to pay for their education. Jack Serunkuma, who played Swiss Cheese, spent a distracted few days trying to find the money to send his brother to a private hospital, the public ones being on strike. There were arrests and bribes to be paid. A public address system, given to the National Theatre by the

Royal Court the year before, was still stuck at Entebbe airport in a tangle of red tape. (Communication between the stage-manager's box and backstage during the performance was either by semaphore or the telephone in Joseph Walugembe's backstage office.) It seemed easier at times to find a mobile phone than a reel of Sellotape, a new drill-bit or a sharp saw. And the rains, though not the biggest problem, were a problem none the less. During the day-long technical rehearsal it became impossible to hear the actors on stage from the second row of the auditorium, so great was the noise of the rain on the corrugated iron roof and the plopping of water into buckets. Yet the company persisted. And part of their energy seemed to lie in their ability to engage with, to be guided rather than handicapped by, their new environment in its destroyed state. Ten years into peace, it is probably more precious because it seems possible.

The peace inside Uganda doesn't feel fragile – although the reaction of the 'twilight girls' to the Independence Day fireworks testifies to the country's lingering insecurity – but problems over recent years in neighbouring Rwanda and Burundi, the genocidal hostility of Tutsi and Hutu, threaten to draw Uganda and the other countries of East Africa back into tribal warfare. As I write, it is reported that 'Tanzania, Uganda and Ethiopia [are] among African countries offering to send . . . what is euphemistically described as security assistance'[47] into Burundi.

Brecht described Mother Courage's inability to learn about the war at the time he wrote the play as 'prophetic'. The Ugandan production of *Maama Nalukalala Ne'zzadde Lye* was not played, or received, as prophecy. For me it was the most passionate anti-war statement I have experienced, passionate in its realism, passionate in its assertion of humanity, passionate in its critique of war.

PRODUCTIONS CITED

Germany

11 January 1949
> Deutsches Theater, Berlin
> DIRECTORS: Brecht and Erich Engel
> DESIGNER: Heinrich Kilger (after Teo Otto)
> MOTHER C: Helene Weigel

8 October 1950
> Kammerspiele, Munich
> DIRECTOR: Brecht
> DESIGNER: Teo Otto
> MOTHER C: Therese Giehse

25 November 1964
> Bühnen der Stadt, Cologne
> DIRECTOR: Peter Palitzsch
> DESIGNER: Bert Kistner
> MOTHER C: Ursula von Reibnitz

12 June 1965
> Ruhrfestspiele, Recklinghausen
> DIRECTOR: Harry Buckwitz
> DESIGNER: Teo Otto
> MOTHER C: Lotte Lenya

3 October 1978
> Theater am Schiffbauerdamm, Berlin
> DIRECTOR: Peter Kupke
> DESIGNER: Manfred Grund
> MOTHER C: Gisela May

27 April 1981
    Schauspielhaus, Bochum
    DIRECTOR: Alfred Kirchner
    DESIGNER: Mariette Eggmann
    MOTHER C: Kirsten Dene

25 May 1986
    Deutsches Schauspielhaus, Hamburg
    DIRECTOR AND DESIGNER: Wilfried Minks
    MOTHER C: Eva Mattes

Switzerland, France and Austria

19 April 1941
    Schauspielhaus, Zürich
    DIRECTOR: Leopold Lindtberg
    DESIGNER: Teo Otto
    MOTHER C: Therese Giehse

17 November 1951
    Théâtre de Suresnes, Paris
    DIRECTOR: Jean Vilar
    MOTHER C: Germaine Montéro

22 February 1963
    Volkstheater, Vienna
    DIRECTOR: Gustav Manker
    DESIGNER: Rudolf Schneider-Manns
    MOTHER C: Dorothea Neff

3 June 1986
    Burgtheater, Vienna
    DIRECTOR: Christoph Schroth
    DESIGNER: Lothar Scharsich
    MOTHER C: Elisabeth Orth

United States of America

17 January 1956
    Marines' Memorial Theatre, San Francisco
    DIRECTOR: Herbert Blau

DESIGNER: Ernest Baron
MOTHER C: Beatrice Manley

28 March 1963
Martin Beck Theatre, New York
DIRECTOR: Jerome Robbins
DESIGNER: Ming Cho Lee
MOTHER C: Anne Bancroft

23 February 1975
Performing Garage, New York
DIRECTOR: Richard Schechner
DESIGNER: Jerry N. Rojo and James Clayburgh
MOTHER C: Joan MacIntosh

United Kingdom

January 1955
Institute of Contemporary Arts, London
DIRECTOR: Eric Capon
MOTHER C: Ina de la Haye

July 1955
Taw and Torridge Festival, Barnstaple
DIRECTOR AND MOTHER C: Joan Littlewood
DESIGNER: (John Bury)

12 May 1965
National Theatre at the Old Vic, London
DIRECTOR: William Gaskill
DESIGNER: Jocelyn Herbert
MOTHER C: Madge Ryan

25 October 1970
Citizens' Theatre, Glasgow
DIRECTOR: Rob Walker
DESIGNER: Philip Prowse
MOTHER C: Ann Mitchell

8 November 1984
> Barbican Centre (Royal Shakespeare Company), London
> DIRECTOR: Howard Davies
> DESIGNER: John Napier
> MOTHER C: Judi Dench

4 May 1990
> Citizens' Theatre, Glasgow
> DIRECTOR AND DESIGNER: Philip Prowse
> MOTHER C: Glenda Jackson

4 November 1995
> Royal National Theatre, London
> DIRECTOR: Jonathan Kent
> DESIGNER: Paul Bond
> MOTHER C: Diana Rigg

Uganda

19 October 1995
> National Theatre, Kampala
> DIRECTORS: Jane Collins and Jessica Kaahwa
> DESIGNERS: Michael Mpyangu and Michael Pavelka
> MOTHER C: Rose Mbowa

Radio, Television and Film

7 December 1955
> BBC Third Programme
> DIRECTOR/PRODUCER: R. D. Smith
> MOTHER C: Maria Fein

30 June 1959
> BBC Television
> DIRECTOR: Rudolph Cartier
> DESIGNER: Clifford Hatts
> MOTHER C: Flora Robson

1961

DEFA Film
DIRECTORS: Peter Palitzsch and Manfred Wekwerth
MOTHER C: Helene Weigel

26 May 1990

BBC Radio Three
DIRECTOR/PRODUCER: Jeremy Mortimer
MOTHER C: Sheila Hancock

NOTES

I SOURCES

1 Brecht, *Letters 1913–1956* (New York: Routledge, 1990), 292.
2 Quoted in Klaus Völker, *Brecht: A Biography* (London: Marion Boyars, 1979), 265.
3 C. V. Wedgwood, *The Thirty Years War* (London: Pimlico edn, 1992), 7.
4 *Ibid.*, 505.
5 *Ibid.*, 512.
6 Grimmelshausen, *Mother Courage* (London: Folio Society, 1965), 8.
7 Friedrich Schiller, *Plays* (Harmondsworth: Penguin Books, 1979), 180–1.
8 *Ibid.*, 185.
9 *Ibid.*
10 *Ibid.*, 204.
11 Brecht, *Letters*, 268.
12 Quoted in *Brecht on Theatre*, trans. John Willett (London: Methuen, 1964), 24.
13 There are significant variations in the English translations of Marx's work. This version is from J. M. Cameron's neglected *Scrutiny of Marxism* (London: SCM Press, 1948), 17.
14 Brecht, *Letters*, 261.
15 *Ibid.*, 205.
16 Brecht, *Journals 1934–1955* (London: Methuen, 1993), 59.
17 Eric Hobsbawm, *Age of Extremes* (London: Michael Joseph, 1994), 52.
18 Brecht, *Journals*, 401.
19 *Ibid.*, 38.
20 *Ibid.*, 47.
21 *Ibid.*, 296.

22 J. B. Morton, *The Barber of Putney* (Harmondsworth: Penguin Books, 1939), 157.
23 *Ibid.*, 9.
24 Brecht, *Journals*, 73.
25 *Ibid.*, 143.
26 *Ibid.*, 501.
27 James K. Lyon, *Bertolt Brecht in America* (Princeton University Press, 1980), 141.
28 *Ibid.*, 149.
29 *Ibid.*, 123.
30 This information is taken from Hobsbawm, *Age of Extremes*, 143.

2 THE TEXT AND THE STAGE

1 Brecht, *Journals*, 34.
2 Quoted in Chester Wilmot, *The Struggle for Europe* (London: Collins, 1952), 82.
3 *Ibid.*, xi.
4 Quoted in Klaus Völker, *Brecht Chronicle* (New York: Seabury Press, 1975), 141–2.
5 Brecht, *Journals*, 56.
6 *Ibid.*, 235.
7 *Ibid.*, 386.
8 *Ibid.*, 403.
9 Brecht's response to this detail of performance is recorded in Berlau, Ruth et al., *Theaterarbeit* (Dresden: Dresdner, 1952), 238.
10 Robert Leach, '*Mother Courage and Her Children*', in *The Cambridge Companion to Brecht*, eds. Peter Thomson and Glendyr Sacks (Cambridge University Press, 1994), 132.
11 Wedgwood, *The Thirty Years War*, 434.
12 Hobsbawm, *Age of Extremes*, 414.
13 See Berlau et al., *Theaterarbeit*, 380.

3 THE BERLIN PRODUCTION: 1949

1 Brecht, *Letters*, 451.
2 Brecht, *Journals*, 404–5.
3 *Ibid.*, 401.
4 *Ibid.*, 411.

5 Andreas Meyer-Hanno, 'Lenya's return to Berlin', *Kurt Weill Newsletter* 3:1 (Spring 1985), 8.

6 Brecht, *Journals*, 399–400.

7 For a full treatment of the Brecht–Lukács debate, see David Pike, *Lukács and Brecht* (Chapel Hill: University of North Carolina Press, 1985).

8 Quoted in Anthony Read and David Fisher, *Berlin: The Biography of a City* (London: Hutchinson, 1994), 273.

9 Brecht, *Journals*, 439.

10 *Ibid.*, 404.

11 The quotation is from a leaflet, on display in Brecht's former house in Berlin, but the substantial work from which it is taken is *Paul Dessau: Dokumente zu Leben und Werk* (Berlin: Akademie der Künste, 1995).

12 See John Willett, *Caspar Neher* (London: Methuen, 1986), 106.

13 Christopher Baugh, 'Brecht and stage design: the Bühnenbildner and the Bühnenbauer', in *The Cambridge Companion to Brecht*, eds. Thomson and Sacks, 235–53.

14 Ekkehard Schall, 'Acting with the Berliner Ensemble', *New Theatre Quarterly* 6 (May 1986), 99.

15 See *Brecht on Theatre*, 283.

16 Brecht, *Journals*, 452.

17 Käthe Rülicke-Weiler, 'Brecht and Weigel at the Berliner Ensemble', *New Theatre Quarterly* 25 (February 1991), 7.

18 Quoted in Margaret Eddershaw, *Performing Brecht* (London: Routledge, 1996), 37.

19 Schall, 'Acting with the Berliner Ensemble', 103.

20 For an important critique of Brecht's *eingreifendes Denken* ('thought that develops with economics constantly in mind'), see David Pike, 'Brecht and "Inoperative Thinking"', in *Critical Essays on Bertolt Brecht*, ed. Siegfried Mews (Boston, Mass.: G. K. Hall & Co., 1989), 257–72.

21 Alain Touraine, *The Return of the Actor* (Minneapolis: University of Minnesota Press, 1988), 139.

22 Brecht, *Journals*, 403.

23 Heinz Kuckhahn, who had worked with Brecht on the film *Kuhle Wampe* in 1931–2, was an assistant in the 1949 production of *Mother Courage*. He was not part of the Berliner Ensemble.

24 Brecht, *Journals*, 409.
25 *Ibid.*, 426.
26 Brecht, *Poems 1913–1956* (London: Eyre Methuen, 1976), 341.
27 *Ibid.*, 427.
28 Brecht, *Journals*, 302.
29 Elizabeth Wright, *Postmodern Brecht: A Re-presentation* (London: Routledge, 1989), 114.
30 I take these timings from D. R. Jones, *Great Directors at Work* (Berkeley: University of California Press, 1986), 131.
31 Brecht, *Journals*, 416–17.
32 *Ibid.*, 284.
33 Wright, *Postmodern Brecht*, 52.
34 Brecht, *Journals*, 415.
35 *Ibid.*, 416.
36 *Ibid.*, 417.
37 *Ibid.*, 404.
38 *Ibid.*, 83.
39 *Ibid.*, 110.
40 *Ibid.*, 453.
41 Meg Mumford, 'Brecht Studies Stanislavski: just a tactical move?', *New Theatre Quarterly* 43 (August 1995), 242.
42 Brecht, *Poems 1913–1956*, 415.
43 Brecht, *Journals*, 377.

4 'MOTHER COURAGE' IN ENGLISH
1 *Tynan on Theatre* (Harmondsworth: Penguin Books, 1964), 230.
2 *Ibid.*, 241.
3 Quoted in Philip Roberts, *The Royal Court Theatre 1965–1972* (London: Routledge, 1986), 17.
4 William Gaskill, *A Sense of Direction* (London: Faber and Faber, 1988), 13.
5 *Ibid.*, 51.
6 Martin Esslin, *Brief Chronicles* (London: Temple Smith, 1970), 88.
7 Gaskill, *A Sense of Direction*, 59.
8 *Ibid.*, 58.
9 *The Cambridge Guide to World Theatre*, ed. Martin Banham (Cambridge University Press, 1988), 1063.

10 Quoted in Roland Rees, *Fringe First* (London: Oberon Books, 1992), 209.

11 Brecht, *Journals*, 186.

12 *Ibid.*, 349.

13 Gaskill, *A Sense of Direction*, 58.

14 This quotation from the RSC programme for *Mother Courage* is cited in a cogent critique of the production by Christopher McCullough in *The Politics of Theatre and Drama*, ed. Graham Holderness (London: Macmillan, 1992), 120–33.

15 Gerald Jacobs, *Judi Dench: A Great Deal of Laughter* (London: Weidenfeld and Nicolson, 1985), 117.

16 McCullough's essay (see note 14, above) details some of the ways in which Brecht's work has been appropriated by a fundamentally unsympathetic theatre.

17 See Rees, *Fringe First*, 209–10.

18 Margaret Eddershaw, *Performing Brecht*, 138.

19 Quoted in Eddershaw, *ibid.*, 134.

20 *Ibid.*

21 The observation is Eddershaw's, *ibid.*, 136.

22 Hare calls the published text (London: Methuen, 1995) 'a version for the National Theatre'. The quoted passage is the conclusion of his Introduction.

23 *Guardian*, 17 November 1995.

24 See note 10, above.

25 *The Times*, 16 November 1995.

26 Brecht, *Collected Plays*, eds. Ralph Manheim and John Willett, vol. v, 167.

27 The passage appears on page 43 of Hare's version (London: Methuen, 1995).

28 Maarten Van Dijk, 'Blocking Brecht', in *Re-interpreting Brecht*, eds. Pia Kleber and Colin Visser (Cambridge University Press, 1990), 118.

29 See Roland Barthes, *The Responsibility of Forms*, trans. Richard Howard (New York: Hill and Wang, 1985), 93.

30 Eddershaw, *Performing Brecht*, 134.

31 Wright, *Postmodern Brecht*, 22.

32 Barthes, 'The Tasks of Brechtian Criticism', trans. Peter W. Mathers, *Theatre Quarterly* 33 (Spring 1979), 27.

33 *Ibid.*, 28.

34 Heiner Müller, *Krieg ohne Schlacht* (Cologne, 1992), 361.

35 Herbert Blau, *The Impossible Theater* (New York: Macmillan, 1964), 205.

36 *Ibid.*, 107.

37 *Ibid.*, 203.

38 *Ibid.*

39 *Ibid.*, 188.

40 *Ibid.*, 195.

41 *Ibid.*, 197.

42 Barthes, 'Réponses', *Tel Quel* 47 (1971), 89–107.

43 *Ibid.*, 95.

44 Blau, *The Impossible Theater*, 196n.

45 *Ibid.*, 19.

46 *American Theatre Companies 1931–1986*, ed. Weldon B. Durham (New York: Greenwood Press, 1989), 33.

47 Blau, *The Impossible Theater*, 200–1.

48 Cheryl Crawford, *One Naked Individual* (Indianapolis/New York: Bobbs Merrill, 1977), 261.

49 *Ibid.*, 262.

50 The seminal text is again 'Réponses' (see note 42, above).

51 Richard Schechner, *Performance Theory* (New York and London: Routledge, 1988), 138.

52 *Ibid.*, 201.

53 Paul Ryder Ryan, 'The Performance Group's *Mother Courage*', *The Drama Review* (T66, June 1975), 88.

54 Quoted in Ryder Ryan, '*Mother Courage*', 83.

55 *Ibid.*, 90.

56 Schechner, *Performance Theory*, 139.

57 *Ibid.*

58 For a brief description of this event, see *The Drama Review* (T67, September 1975). This quotation is from p. 75.

59 Quoted in Paul Ryder Ryan, '*Mother Courage*', 82.

5 'MOTHER COURAGE' IN THE GERMANIES AND IN FRANCE

1 Letter to the author, July 1996.

2 Brecht, *Letters*, 496.

3 Brecht, *Journals*, 431.

4 *Ibid.*

5 I take the figures from Michael Patterson, *German Theatre Today* (London: Pitman, 1976), 114–17.

6 Peter Palitzsch's essay on his Cologne production is illustrated by photographs of the full stage for each of the twelve scenes. This quotation is from p. 60 of *Theater Heute* (January 1965).

7 Paul Kruntorad, *Theater Heute* (June 1986), 54.

8 Klaus Völker, 'Productions of Brecht's plays on the West German stage, 1945–1986', in *Re-interpreting Brecht*, eds. Kleber and Visser, 72.

9 *Ibid.*, 73.

10 Quoted in Donald Spoto, *Lenya: A Life* (Boston, Mass./Toronto: Little, Brown and Company, 1989), 276.

11 Werner Mittenzwei, *Wer war Brecht?* (Berlin: Aufbau, 1977), 100.

12 Hobsbawm, *Age of Extremes*, 579.

13 Berliner Ensemble, *Mutter Courage und ihre Kinder*, Theaterarbeit in der DDR 5 (Berlin: Brecht-Zentrum der DDR, 1981), 42.

14 *Ibid.*, 10.

15 *Ibid.*, 46.

16 Brecht, *Journals*, 98.

17 *Ibid.*, 280.

18 Berliner Ensemble, *Mutter Courage* (1981), 65.

19 John Willett, *The Theatre of Erwin Piscator* (London: Eyre Methuen, 1978).

20 Jean Caune, *La Culture en action: de Vilar à Lang* (Grenoble: Presses Universitaires de Grenoble, 1992), 83.

21 I am quoting from the collection of observations on the Théâtre National Populaire, published in *Theatre Quarterly* 23 (Autumn 1976), 53.

22 *Ibid.*

23 *Tynan on Theatre*, 204.

24 Jean Vilar, writing in *Les Lettres Françaises* (9 June 1960).

25 Bernard Dort, writing in *Les Temps Modernes* (1960), cited in Agnes Hüfner, *Brecht in Frankreich* 1930–1963 (Stuttgart: Metzlersche, 1968), 17.

26 *Tynan on Theatre*, 202.

27 See *Ten Talents in the American Theatre*, ed. David H. Stephens (Norman, Okla.: University of Oklahoma Press, 1957), 101.

28 David Bradby, *Modern French Drama 1940–1980* (Cambridge University Press, 1984), 94.

29 Quoted in *The Cambridge Guide to World Theatre*, ed. Banham, 988.

30 Bernard Dort, 'Crossing the desert: Brecht in France in the eighties', in *Re-interpreting Brecht*, eds. Kleber and Visser, 103.

31 Fiona Shaw in discussion with Roland Rees, in Rees, *Fringe First*, 164.

6 THE AFTERLIFE OF 'MOTHER COURAGE'

1 John Drakakis, 'The essence that's not seen: the radio adaptation of stage plays', in *Radio Drama*, ed. Peter Lewis (London: Longman, 1981), 128.

2 Thomas Elsaesser, 'From anti-illusionism to hyper-realism: Bertolt Brecht and contemporary film', in *Re-interpreting Brecht*, eds. Kleber and Visser, 172.

3 Kim H. Kowalke, 'Brecht and music: theory and practice', in *The Cambridge Companion to Brecht*, eds. Thomson and Sacks, 226.

4 See Chapter 4, note 42, above.

5 Peter Brook, *The Empty Space* (Harmondsworth: Penguin Books, 1972), 86.

6 Peter Brook, *The Shifting Point* (London: Methuen, 1988), 42.

7 *The Book of US* (London: Calder and Boyars, 1968), 17.

8 Brook, *Empty Space*, 80–81.

9 *The Book of US*, 10.

10 Brook, *Empty Space*, 81.

11 Brook, *Shifting Point*, 61.

12 *The Book of US*, 190–91.

13 *Ibid.*, 137.

14 Brook, *Shifting Point*, 62.

15 *The Book of US*, 214.

16 *Ibid.*, 138.

17 *Ibid.*, 188.

18 *Ibid.*, 192.

19 *Ibid.*, 132.

20 *Ibid.*, 188.

21 *Ibid.*, 195.

22 *Ibid.*, 197.

23 Brecht, *Journals*, 103.

24 Paul Green, 'Symphonic drama: a narrative of reminiscence', in *Ten Talents in the American Theatre*, ed. Stephens, 257.

25 Quoted in *Kurt Weill*: The Threepenny Opera, ed. Stephen Hinton (Cambridge University Press, 1990), 89.

26 Berliner Ensemble, *Mutter Courage* (1981), 42.

27 George Colman the Younger, *Random Records* (London, 1830), vol. II, 93.

28 Brecht, *Journals*, 120.

29 For an edited version of the interview from which this quotation is drawn, see *The Playwrights Speak*, ed. Walter Wager (London: Longman, 1969), 206.

30 Quoted in Frances Gray, *John Arden* (London: Macmillan, 1982), 4.

31 John Arden, *Plays: One* (London: Eyre Methuen, 1977), 35.

32 Gray, *John Arden*, 3.

33 Quoted in *Il Messagero* (29 June 1996), 21.

34 Graham Ackroyd, *The Forests Are Burning* (Hove: Lansdowne Press, 1996).

35 For translation and comments on this play, I am indebted to Lesley Soule. Her translation is scheduled for publication in Slovenia in 1996–7.

36 Unpublished diary of the production's co-designer, Michael Pavelka.

37 Unpublished diary of the production's co-director, Jane Collins.

38 Brecht, 'On Everyday Theatre', in *Poems 1913–1956*, 176.

39 The extract is from Brecht's essay 'The Street Scene'. See *Brecht on Theatre*, 126–7.

40 Viv Gardner notes: 'I write with some hesitation about the music as I am no musicologist, let alone an African musicologist. I can describe its effect, but only offer a tentative analysis of how it achieved that effect.'

41 Viv Gardner notes: 'The extent of the religious rather than tribal dimension in the Ugandan civil conflict came as a complete revelation to me.' For further information, see Thomas P. Ofcansky, *Uganda: Tarnished Pearl of Africa* (Oxford: Westview Press, 1996) and Phares Mutibwa, *Uganda since Independence* (London: Hurst and Company, 1992).

42 The majority of those involved in the production were either Baganda or had lived and worked in Buganda during the civil war. In Buganda alone, during the second period of Obote's government, 'conservative estimates are that 300,000 people may have been killed and another 500,000 displaced . . . Soldiers and other agents of the regime were turned by the system into instruments to wipe out a whole nationality' (Mutibwa, *Uganda since Independence*, 159).

43 This suggestion is made in notes translated into English in *Encore* (May/June 1965), 44.

44 Brecht, 'Weigel's Props', in *Poems 1913–1956*, 427.

45 Viv Gardner notes: 'As stage-manager for the performance, drafted in when the UK stage-manager, Dougie Wilson, broke his arm, I was on the side of the Ugandans, as I had to deal with an increasingly foetid carcass.' Joan Littlewood described to me, in December 1995, how she experienced nausea over the carcass of the capon in Barnstaple.

46 Ofcansky, *Uganda*, 58.

47 *Guardian*, 8 July 1996.

SELECT BIBLIOGRAPHY

Books, articles and reviews quoted in the text are fully annotated in the notes to individual chapters. This short bibliography is confined to books which contain material with a direct bearing on the staging of *Mother Courage and Her Children.*

BRECHT IN TRANSLATION
Mother Courage and Her Children, trans. Ralph Manheim, in *Collected Plays*, eds. Ralph Manheim and John Willett, vol. V (New York: Vintage Books, 1972). This is the translation I have favoured in quoting from the text. It includes (pp. 331–401) important notes from the *Couragemodell.*
Poems 1913–1956, eds. John Willett and Ralph Manheim (London: Eyre Methuen, 1976).
Brecht on Theatre, trans. John Willett (London: Methuen, 1964).
Journals 1934–1955, trans. Hugh Rorrison (London: Methuen, 1993).
Letters 1913–1956, trans. Ralph Manheim (New York: Routledge, 1990).

MATERIAL ON THE PLAY IN GERMAN
Berlau, Ruth et al., *Theaterarbeit* (Dresden: Dresdner, 1952). A record in words and photographs of the early productions of the Berliner Ensemble. A later edition (Frankfurt: Suhrkamp, 1961) provides a photographic record of six productions. Even for those with no German, *Theaterarbeit* is a valuable resource.
Brecht, Bertolt, *Couragemodell* (Berlin: Henschelverlag, 1958).
Hecht, Werner, *Materialen zu Brechts* Mutter Courage und ihre Kinder (Frankfurt: Suhrkamp, 1964).

Hof, Gert, Mutter Courage und ihre Kinder *von Bertolt Brecht: eine Dokumentation der Aufführung des Berliner Ensembles 1978* (Berlin: Brecht-Zentrum der DDR, 1981).

Tenschert, Joachim, Mutter Courage und ihre Kinder*: Bühnenfassung des Berliner Ensembles* (Berlin: Henschelverlag, 1968).

SECONDARY SOURCES

Barthes, Roland, *Image-Music-Text* (London: Fontana, 1977).

Bartram, Graham and Anthony Waine, eds., *Brecht in Perspective* (London: Longman, 1982).

Blau, Herbert, *The Impossible Theater* (New York: Macmillan, 1964).

Bradby, David, *Modern French Drama 1940–1980* (Cambridge University Press, 1984).

Bradby, David and John McCormick, *People's Theatre* (London: Croom Helm, 1978).

Brooker, Peter, *Bertolt Brecht: Dialectics, Poetry, Politics* (London: Croom Helm, 1988).

Dickson, Keith, *Towards Utopia: A Study of Brecht* (Oxford: Clarendon Press, 1978).

Eddershaw, Margaret, *Performing Brecht: Forty Years of British Performances* (London: Routledge, 1996).

Fuegi, John, *Bertolt Brecht: Chaos According to Plan* (Cambridge University Press, 1987).

Jones, David R., *Great Directors at Work* (Berkeley: University of California Press, 1986).

Kleber, Pia and Colin Visser, eds., *Re-interpreting Brecht: His Influence on Contemporary Drama and Film* (Cambridge University Press, 1990).

Mews, Siegfried, ed., *Critical Essays on Bertolt Brecht* (Boston, Mass.: G. K. Hall & Co., 1989).

Mitter, Shomit, *Systems of Rehearsal* (London: Routledge, 1992).

Needle, Jan and Peter Thomson, *Brecht* (Oxford: Basil Blackwell, 1981).

Rees, Roland, *Fringe First* (London: Oberon Books, 1992).

Schechner, Richard, *Performance Theory* (New York and London: Routledge, 1988).

Thomson, Peter and Glendyr Sacks, *The Cambridge Companion to Brecht* (Cambridge University Press, 1994).

Witt, Hubert, ed., *Brecht As They Knew Him* (London: Lawrence & Wishart, 1975).

INDEX